LEADING WITH AUTHENTICITY IN TIMES OF TRANSITION

Center for Creative Leadership

NORTH AMERICA EUROPE ASIA

www.ccl.org

The Center for Creative Leadership is an international, nonprofit educational institution founded in 1970 to advance the understanding, practice, and development of leadership for the benefit of society worldwide. As a part of this mission, it publishes books and reports that aim to contribute to a general process of inquiry and understanding in which ideas related to leadership are raised, exchanged, and evaluated. The ideas presented in its publications are those of the author or authors.

The Center thanks you for supporting its work through the purchase of this volume. If you have comments, suggestions, or questions about any CCL Press publication, please contact the Director of Publications at the address given below.

Center for Creative Leadership
Post Office Box 26300
Greensboro, North Carolina 27438-6300
Telephone 336 288 7210
www.ccl.org

Kerry A. Bunker
Michael Wakefield

LEADING WITH
AUTHENTICITY
IN TIMES OF
TRANSITION

CENTER FOR CREATIVE LEADERSHIP
Greensboro, North Carolina

CCL Stock No. 188
©2005 Center for Creative Leadership

Published by CCL Press
Martin Wilcox, Director of Publications
Peter Scisco, Editor, CCL Press
Karen Mayworth, Associate Editor
Joanne Ferguson, Production Editor

Cover design by Joanne Ferguson

Library of Congress Cataloging-in-Publication Data

Bunker, Kerry A.
     Leading with authenticity in times of transition / Kerry Bunker and Michael
Wakefield.
          p. cm.
     ISBN 1-882197-88-7
   1. Organizational change. 2. Industrial management. 3. Leadership.
I. Wakefield, Michael. II. Title.
     HD58.8.B864 2005
     658.4'092—dc22

                                                                   2004062932

CONTENTS

PREFACE

Change and transition are no longer periodic events. Today, they are the ongoing and natural state of many organizations. Economic, political, technological, cultural, and societal factors all contribute to the pace and complexity of change. Through our work, we have seen the ways many senior-level managers effect change and respond to it, orchestrating processes and leading the people around them. What has become clear is that many of them are highly skilled in leading and managing the structural side of change: creating a vision, reorganizing, restructuring, and so on. But rarely do managers fully grasp or focus on the human side of change: grieving, letting go, building hope, and learning. And when leaders do pay attention to the deeper emotions and behaviors tied to difficult change, few know how to appropriately address those emotions and behaviors.

We wrote this book as a way to bring focus and insight to the human side of leadership in times of transition, and to do so in a way that would be useful to managers and executives. Much has been written about how to manage change—the structural elements of change that are based on business acumen—but in our experience, these books rarely help managers sort through the human dynamics of transition. Even the best-selling book *Who Moved My Cheese?* (which depicts the emotional reality of change and transition) doesn't help leaders navigate the complexity that emerges when the emotional side of transition is combined with the business demands of change. We hope leaders will identify with the pressures, the trade-offs, and the challenges we describe, and then use this book to ask, "What is getting in the way of my ability to lead effectively, and what can I do about it?"

Learning how individuals and organizations cope and adapt during times of change and transition has been part of our work for many years, both at the Center for Creative Leadership and in prior training and development roles (Kerry at AT&T, Michael at BellSouth). At CCL, we've worked for more than fifteen years designing and conducting customized leadership development programs for organizations, including systemic initiatives spanning several years. While there are many books, strategic consultants, and executive training workshops dedicated to change management, few if any answer the crucial question that change poses: how do leaders in real settings with real people help themselves and others work their way through difficult times?

We've found that the answer—though complex and demanding—is grounded in the authenticity of leaders and hinges on trust.

Building trust requires leaders to be honest and genuine. In today's changing times, the most authentic, effective leaders find a way to address the emotions of transition. Authentic leaders can effectively deal with the structural challenges of change and guide people through the transition that accompanies change.

This book is for senior-level practicing managers and those who work with them—human resources professionals, coaches, consultants—indeed, entire management teams. In it, we present a framework for understanding the competencies required to respond to the demands of maintaining the business while attending to the equally important "people" concerns. We hope to provide insight for leaders so that they can decipher and adjust their behavior to maintain the crucial balance between the structural side of leading change and the human side of leading transition.

We wish to extend special thanks to a number of individuals whose support, encouragement, insight, and collaborative wisdom made this work possible. I, Kerry, thank my wife, Sheri, whose wisdom, instinct, and commonsense reflections on leadership and authenticity never cease to amaze me. She is my partner and sounding board, and the centering force that helps our children and me strive for a healthy balance of the paradoxical competencies required to navigate our own life transitions. And I, Michael, am forever beholden to Johnson, Beauty, and the Beast—affectionate pseudonyms for my wife, Joyce, and our children, Niki and Dylan. I recognize them as my most important teachers.

As this book reflects on lessons learned primarily from the practice of leadership development rather than from academic models of research, there are numerous fellow travelers who deserve recognition for their special roles in shaping our thinking along the way. We were blessed to be making this incredible journey with an extraordinary band of talented professionals. They shared in the trials, tribulations, and triumphs that seem to be part and parcel of helping leaders learn to be resilient and effective in the face of the many challenges that threaten to erode both trust and authenticity. First, we want to acknowledge the core team that was largely responsible for catalyzing the learning process over the course of ten years and nearly one hundred offerings of the Leading Transitions intervention—first with the Canadian Federal Public Service and later with the United States Postal Service. Specifically, we want to thank Jim Shields, Carole Leland, Beth Dixson, Amy Webb, and Ted Dougherty (as well as the expanded team of facilitators who joined us at various stages) for their professionalism, insight, and passionate commitment.

We are also indebted to our equally passionate internal partners in those two organizations: Dan Burke, Paul Robilliard, Michel Bourdon, and Carolyn Cyr in the Canadian Government, and Bill Stefl and Olaf Jaehnigen at the Postal Service. We stand in awe of the more than two thousand executives who accepted the risk of diving deeply into an emotionally charged learning experience with us—simply because they were committed to their organizations and to helping themselves and each other grow and develop, both as authentic leaders and as genuine human beings.

We would be remiss if we failed to acknowledge the support and contributions of the entire team at CCL, including administration, testing, and support services. We especially want to express gratitude for the commitment and hard work of Jenni Maxson and Betty Williams, and for the ongoing support of David Altman and John Fleenor in the continuing research.

Over the years our thinking has been influenced by a number of thought leaders in the areas of learning, change, and transition, including William Bridges, Barry Johnson, Cynthia Scott and Dennis Jaffe, Daniel Goleman, Cary Cherniss, Mary Lynn Pulley, and David Noer. As our work continues, we are also finding fruitful linkages and related frameworks in the research and development efforts of Robert E. Kaplan and Rob Kaiser.

Finally, we wish to acknowledge the invaluable assistance, guidance, and support of Rebecca Garau, Pete Scisco, and Karen Mayworth in helping us bring this manuscript to completion.

INTRODUCTION

Organizations today are awash in change. The change may come from within, such as a downsizing or an expansion, but more likely it's driven by external factors, such as holding the lead in a market or struggling in one.

The challenge of leading organizations through change goes beyond setting strategy, making plans, and implementing the structures and processes of change. Often the real struggle lies in managing the long-term aspects of recovery, revitalization, and recommitment. In other words, the significant work of managing change requires leaders to focus simultaneously on managing the business and providing effective leadership to the people. More often than not, it is the focus on the people side of leadership that loses out.

The risk leaders face in minimizing or ignoring the human dynamic that plays out in the context of change and transition is twofold. First, they may prevent or undermine the organization's structural and strategic goals by failing to gain sufficient buy-in and commitment from employees. Second, they may destabilize the organization's culture and erode the trust and values that engender dedication. Loyalty and trust give way to insecurity and fear, while productivity and enthusiasm are displaced by withdrawal and skepticism.

In our work with organizations, we help leaders examine their individual styles and approaches as well as the underlying emotional dynamics that play out in times of change. In this book, we offer a framework for understanding the issues and competencies that contribute to effective leadership during times of change. Our purpose is to help leaders determine how to choose and move among a variety of managerial approaches, to help them see what's working, what's not working, and what's missing. In this way, leaders can more clearly assess their impact and learn how to meet the demands of both managing the business and leading the people.

Our experience with more than three thousand leaders in multiple organizations underscores that in order for leaders to effectively harness and maintain the talent and commitment needed to benefit from organizational change, they must

- Examine their behaviors and emotions tied to change and transition. This begins the process of operating from a place of authenticity as a leader. These questions get at the heart of how one leads during change and transition: Do I make everything equally urgent? Do I avoid ambiguity or downplay uncertainty? Do I feel overwhelmed or isolated? Am I overly optimistic, to the point of raising questions about whether I'm in touch with the real challenges? Am I too attached to protecting my people? Do I bully others when I feel anxious or impatient?

- Establish and protect trust. Without trust and honesty, authenticity and credibility suffer—undermining otherwise solid change initiatives or management decisions. Leaders are well served by honestly assessing trust: Do I trust those around me? Do they trust me? Is there a culture of trust or distrust in the organization?

- Find a balance between structural leadership and people leadership. By learning the important competencies for leading in times of change and transition (we discuss twelve in this book), leaders gain a new perspective from which to operate. They can then identify which of the competencies they exaggerate, which ones they minimize or ignore, and in which areas they strike an effective balance. From this diagnosis, leaders can employ new leadership strategies.

By presenting a framework for understanding these issues, describing specific competencies, illustrating them in a real way, and providing tips and tactics for their use, this book will assist managers who are charged with leading themselves and others in a constantly changing workplace.

1

BUILDING TRUST IN EXTRAORDINARY TIMES

Consider three people:

Rachel is a vice president of sales and marketing for a Fortune 50 company. The company recruited her a year ago in large part because of her impressive track record with its top competitor. Her move was the result of years of hard work and patience, and from Rachel's perspective it was a well-deserved reward. She had finally earned a senior-level job at a powerful company, had creative and talented management teams to lead, and was eager to enjoy all the perks of hitting the corporate big time.

But all is not well. Rachel is struggling to meet sales and revenue goals, a major initiative to reorganize the global sales force has run aground, the new advertising campaign has garnered luke-warm response, and employee turnover has accelerated in recent months. Rachel is angry, confused, and frustrated at what she perceives to be a lack of commitment from the people in her marketing department, who in her words "won't get with the program," and from salespeople who are resisting the changes she is implementing.

Antonio is the top administrator in a state office of health and human services. Trained in social work, he spent just two years as a caseworker before moving into an administrative role. Antonio has become a skilled manager and effective politician, able to maneuver effectively through local, state, and federal bureaucracies. He's well liked, and he has considered running for public office. But his political ambitions are on hold because he currently faces the toughest challenge of his career. Because of budget shortfalls and pressure for smaller, leaner government operations, Antonio is orchestrating a massive reorganization of his agency that involves a major reduction of employees. As a savvy administrator, Antonio knows what needs to be done, and he's working hard to figure out the best way to do it.

Even though he's the architect of most of the change, Antonio is increasingly anxious about his ability to make it happen. He feels it's important, as he puts it, to "put a good face on the change" and to demonstrate "100 percent commitment to the direction we're headed." Usually very social and engaging, Antonio has kept to himself lately. Uncharacteristically, he's been lashing out when anyone questions his tactics. He feels burned out and is considering leaving public service after the reorganization.

Mitchell was the director of R & D for a small, highly successful biotech firm that was recently purchased by a major pharmaceutical company. A key driver behind the purchase was the perceived value of the smaller firm's work. Mitchell and his colleagues were relieved to learn that they would remain as an intact unit in the larger organization and that no one would be laid off. Even so, the transition has not gone as well as expected. After a three-month honeymoon, company headquarters and the company's main R & D unit started to make noises about how Mitchell's group needs to change its focus.

Mitchell finds himself as the go-between, supporting and speaking for "his" people while negotiating the new environment. He and his R & D team sometimes miss the days when they could just "do the work and not worry about politics," as he describes it. Mitchell is eager to make the transition successful. He's willing to explore the implications and benefits of changing course, but he's also comfortable pushing back and speaking openly to the powers that be in the parent company. He thinks the situation will get better when his colleagues stop comparing the present circumstances to the past. He also realizes that his team needs more time to find its legs so that it can stand up to outside influences and have a more powerful voice in the debate.

Leadership in Extraordinary Times

The leadership pressures that managers like Rachel, Antonio, and Mitchell face are characteristic of current organizational life. Certainly, a crisis or a difficult situation creates extraordinary pressure on organizations and their leaders. But those special circumstances are not required for the emotional pitch of a leadership situation to be shifted. Rachel's new high-profile role, Antonio's restructuring initiative, the acquisition of Mitchell's company—these kinds of events take leaders out of their emotional comfort zone. Leaders face intense pressure to achieve results, putting new expectations and tough demands on themselves and their organizations. In addition, countless sources strain the overall working environment: the economy, unemployment, pressure to do more with less, new challenges of working globally, post-9/11 domestic and international concerns, rapid technological advances, and so on. The reality is that the nature of leadership today is, by and large, bound up in the lurch and sway of change and transition—what we call extraordinary times.

Paradoxically, the dynamic of extraordinary times in organizations is becoming commonplace. Most organizations are experiencing waves of change, one upon another upon another. And their people must make the transition from one organizational reality to the next, over and over again. Managers are so steeped in change as the norm that often when we ask them, "How are you handling the change?" they reply, "Which one? What change are you talking about? There are so many." Rapid, repeated change and constant transition create an emotional dynamic in organizations. Individuals and organizations are running at a higher emotional pitch than they have in decades past.

So what is the impact of extraordinary times on leaders and leadership?

The primary impact is that leading is categorically different when people's emotions are stretched and stressed. Extraordinary times make it both more critical and more difficult for executives to focus simultaneously on managing the business and providing effective leadership. More often than not, it is the focus on the people side of leadership that loses out.

Many managers have mastered the structural side of leading change: creating a vision, reorganizing, setting strategy, restructuring, and so on. They are educated, evaluated, and rewarded on the basis of their dealing with structural challenges and so have more experience with that aspect of organizational change. But they commonly overlook the human side of change—what people need to let go, to build hope, and to learn. That's not to say that these managers are not aware of the human side of change, but too often they don't lead their people in a way that reflects their understanding. Unlike structural changes, which can be handled in an abstract and detached way, the human side of change has to be addressed from the inside out. It is precisely because of the extraordinary changes, stresses, and pressures generated by structural or operational changes that people's needs for leadership are greater. The real challenge to leaders in this position lies in managing the long-term aspects of recovery, revitalization, and recommitment.

Leaders often tell us they would like to pay greater attention to the emotional or human elements of leading change, but they see those as secondary when compared to the more tangible, bottom-line business practices and demands that also require their attention and leadership. But in fact, leaders who minimize or ignore the powerful emotional undercurrents that accompany change and transition risk the bottom line. Perfectly good strategies and change initiatives stall or fail when employees are not committed and engaged. Leaders who fail to gain sufficient buy-in from employees by connecting with their emotional dynamic slow and undermine their progress toward new goals. They may also destabilize the organizational culture by eroding the trust and values that establish and maintain employee dedication. Instead of a loyal, productive, and enthusiastic workforce, executives and managers must lead employees who are insecure, fearful, and skeptical. Their employees are compliant but not committed. And commitment is necessary to make a successful transition.

Valuing Authenticity

We've disappointed managers who have turned to us for a simple diagnosis and five-step program for effective leadership in extraordinary times. We've frustrated HR professionals seeking the big tool or the research-proven quick fix for organizational malaise. We've let down executive teams looking to jump-start a change initiative that has stalled. All of them and many others come to us looking for best practices, saying, "Just tell us what to do." And we tell them that there is a better way to approach both the structural and people sides of an organization in transition. It's potentially more powerful, more far-reaching, and more hopeful than any prepackaged kit of best practices. We also tell them that it is challenging, it is ongoing, and it begins with a focus on leadership not as a way of practice, but as a way of being authentic and straightforward amid the emotional sway of change. Authenticity in a leader generates trust from others. Trust is an elusive quality, but in its absence almost nothing is possible. From a position of trust, a leader can more effectively guide others through change and transition.

Building authenticity into your leadership requires that you see both yourself and others as the complex, whole people you are—emotions included. This perspective takes into account that, during times of change, you and everyone else in the organization are collectively steering a course through the events that surround you, but all of you are navigating individually and in the context of your own lives.

Who you are and what you bring to a situation make a big difference in how you deal with that situation. When different people are faced with the exact same set of circumstances, they are likely to respond in different ways. As a leader, your ability to appreciate that and to lead people with that in mind is an important part of leading effectively in extraordinary times.

Self-awareness and a focus on learning underlie authenticity. Certainly, managers and executives should recognize their strengths and weaknesses. But authenticity calls for a deeper recognition and a closer attention to your emotions, expectations, struggles, motivations, preferences, frustrations—even the contradictions they may hold. Leading with authenticity flows from this foundation of self-knowledge and embraces a commitment to learning. Those who lead with authenticity recognize that what they need to learn about themselves, their organizations, and others is continual, and they find ways to learn and grow through feedback, action, experience, and reflection. In times of change, people look for leaders who can appreciate their vulnerability and inspire them, understand them, support them, and guide them through the valley of chaos. Leaders can meet those needs by being genuine and vulnerable, traits that are themselves powerful learning triggers.

Change and Transition

Change and transition are not the same thing. Transition represents the psychological and emotional adaptation to change. In our work situations, as well as other areas of our lives, adaptation is essentially a process of letting go of the old way and accepting the new way. Leaders need to recognize that when change initiatives are not going well, it is probably because people are stuck in some part of the transition. They may not be ready to let go because what they have to leave behind was comfortable and it worked. They may not be ready to accept because learning is never pain free—there is a drop in competency and comfort at the initial stage of the learning curve. People resist when they feel at risk. They are grieving because they are letting go of something they value and are trying to adapt to something that is unknown. When people feel this way, they aren't able to fully appreciate and to actively commit to a change initiative. Trying to solve the problem by focusing only on the structural side of leadership—reiterating your plans and rationale, pushing the data or measurements—doesn't help resolve the troubles that are connected to people's difficulty with transition. Instead, your leadership task is to connect to the personal and the emotional fallout of change so that you can help individuals in the organization let go, deal with the discomfort, rebuild, and learn.

Leading Change

Here's what frequently happens in an organization when a change initiative is put into play: Accustomed to the structural side of leadership—visioning, reengineering, reorganizing, and restructuring—senior leaders see problems and opportunities, and come up with ways for the organization to deal with them. Skilled managers look at direction, structure, operations, and other factors, and then develop a plan of action. Goals are set, processes are revamped, jobs

ORGANIZATIONAL CHANGE AND TRANSITION

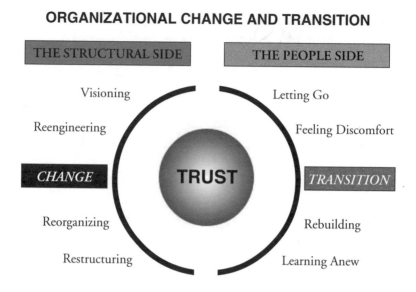

are redesigned or eliminated, and new metrics are established—all under the umbrella of "change initiative." All the while, leaders often mask their own emotional response to the change in an effort to maintain an image of strength.

Then, with some recognition of the importance of commitment and communication, the organization's leaders roll out the new plan/process/structure/strategy. For a large-scale change, announcements, meetings, newsletters, and other communication channels become part of the process. When the situation involves more modest or narrowly focused changes, the organization's leaders often make them with little or no notice and with little or no awareness of unintended consequences. When communication occurs, it is driven by or tuned to legal ramifications.

Having introduced the new way of work, the leaders who are responsible for the plan or for catalyzing the change are usually ready to move on—or they feel compelled to act as if they are ready to move on. They have a plan, they know what to measure, and they know how to proceed. Most managers are focused on leading the structural side of change, represented by the left side of the diagram on the preceding page. That's how leadership has been defined for them, and what they've been rewarded for.

Unfortunately, the best-laid plans for organizational change are frequently diluted or damaged by a failure to exert strong leadership around the people issues. Sooner or later, leaders see that the change isn't working according to plan. Individuals are not performing as needed and are even resistant. In response, leaders naturally turn to their strengths and habitual ways of behaving. They reiterate the logic of the change and push people harder. They try to motivate people by cheerleading, getting angry, threatening. They get impatient when employees won't get with the program. Frustration grows as leaders wonder why employees can't just do what needs to be done. Usually, the organization sheds the more resistant employees, which raises the pressure on and anxiety in the people who remain.

Over the years, we've observed this scenario repeat itself time and time again. Senior leaders from multinational corporations, government agencies, small and midsize businesses, and nonprofit organizations have come to us for help when they hit this point and did not realize the benefits they had expected to see. Our diagnosis of the symptoms is often the same: change initiatives break down because people stall somewhere during the transition.

Leading Transition

Organizational events—restructuring, mergers and acquisitions, and financial difficulty—as well as overall uncertainty trigger all kinds of behavioral and emotional reactions. Confronted by change, people go through a time of transition. This adaptive process occurs at a different pace and in various ways for each individual, depending upon the circumstances. In an organization undergoing change, the leader's responsibility is to live through this process of transition with others in a genuine and authentic way, and to lead in a way that helps bring people through transition so that they can adapt and contribute in the long term.

Leaders who are best able to cope with transition are in touch with their personal reactions to change. They are comfortable sharing those emotions. But such leaders are not the norm. Most leaders have focused little attention on understanding and learning from their own emotional transitions and therefore are not well prepared to foster such efforts in others. When leaders have reservations, a sense of loss, fear, or some other emotion tied to change and their role in it, they need to pay attention to that emotion. Otherwise, they limit their ability to lead with authenticity and to help others cope and adapt.

Building Trust

Even managers who do recognize the emotional power that transition exerts over both them and those they lead rarely have a framework or starting point for coping with the transition. Leaders are most effective in times of transition when they incorporate both structure- and people-related behaviors into their roles and responsibilities. By striking the right balance between the two, leaders build and reinforce trust—a core ingredient for effective leadership.

Without trust from others, leaders can get, at best, a degree of compliance. But only with trust can they elicit genuine commitment from people, particularly during stressful, uncertain times. The challenge of creating an environment of trust is rooted in how difficult it is to earn that trust and how easy it is to damage it.

Leading with authenticity in times of transition isn't a process of checking off a list of steps or tasks, or of saying the right words.

Authenticity: A Foundation of Leadership

Authenticity in a leader generates trust from others. And from a position of trust, a leader can more effectively guide others through change and transition. We've identified three steps you can take to begin to grow as an authentic leader in extraordinary times.

1. Examine your mental models. In *The Fifth Discipline* (1990), Peter Senge writes, "Mental models are deeply ingrained assumptions, generalizations, or even pictures or images that influence how we understand the world and how we take action." We all have mental models of leadership that have become part of our habitual patterns of thinking, perceiving, and behaving. By becoming aware of your assumptions about leadership, you can make conscious choices about how you want to operate as a leader. If these assumptions are left unexamined, however, you repeat patterns that may or may not be serving you well, especially during challenging times.

2. Understand that change is not transition. In *The Way of Transition* (2001), William Bridges describes change as a new way of doing something, transition as the psychological adaptation to the change. Bridges explains that transition starts with an ending. Rather than immediately getting on with the new circumstances, people face a period of adaptation. Leaders need to realize that the transition process involves a time of difficulty, often fraught with self-doubt, ambiguity, and uncertainty. People may be reluctant to accept the reality that something is ending, refusing to let go of the familiar and learn about the new. When you or someone in the organization is struggling with change, take time to

acknowledge transition by exploring what has been lost and what is getting in the way of adapting.

3. Improve your ability to learn. Most of what you need to know about leading through transition you will learn from experience. If you can learn and adapt (and help others to do so), not only will you recover from change and loss, but you can actually thrive. By becoming a more versatile learner, you increase your capacity to cope with change, adapt through transition, and move on to what's next.

It's about looking inward and seeing honestly how your personality, behaviors, and emotions play out as you take on a leadership role. It's about valuing and building trust, understanding the dynamics of change and transition, and discovering openness and vulnerability. Next, we turn to specific leadership competencies that help leaders make these concepts real.

Keeping True: Leadership Competencies for Extraordinary Times

We often use the image of a bicycle wheel to describe the leadership competencies that are important during times of transition. On a bicycle wheel, each spoke needs to be tightened or loosened to the right tension. Otherwise, there will be strain on the other spokes, pulling the wheel out of alignment and making the bike much more difficult to ride. Avid cyclists keep their bikes rolling at top performance by "truing" their wheels—adjusting the tension of the spokes—as part of their routine bicycle maintenance.

Imagine, now, a wheel that has trust as its hub. Radiating out from that hub are the spokes, which represent twelve competencies

TRANSITION LEADERSHIP WHEEL

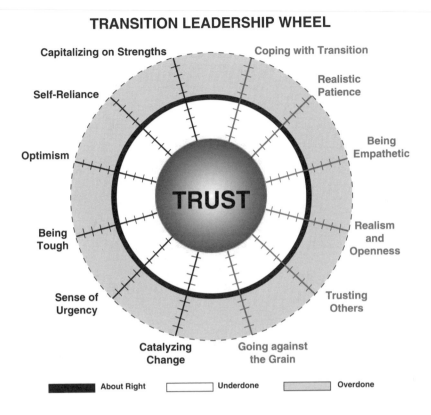

that support authentic, effective leadership in times of transition. Six spokes represent structural competencies; the other six represent people-related competencies. Any of the twelve competencies can be overdone, underdone, or held in a positive, dynamic balance (as the spokes on a bicycle wheel are set in a balanced tension). If a leader neglects or devotes an overabundance of energy to any one element, he or she runs the risk of skewing the opposite, pushing the wheel out of true and creating undue strain on the trust needed to lead effectively during extraordinary times.

It's easy to get out of true—in both cycling and leadership. But while a cyclist can stop riding to fix a wheel, leaders have no choice but to make adjustments as changes swirl around them—in the middle of the ride, so to speak. Adding to their difficulty is the fact that experience and its lessons are coupled with personal preferences to exaggerate or downplay various leadership practices. This often pushes leaders toward emphasizing just three or four leadership competencies—usually the ones that they have been schooled in, the ones organizations reinforce and reward. As a rule, those competencies fall on the structural side of change management. When leaders pay less attention to the people side of change, the tension between the two sides of the wheel can slip out of balance and negatively impact their effectiveness, how they are perceived, and the trust they require to guide people through the phases of transition.

Oftentimes, people are hypersensitive during times of stress and threat. Using our metaphor of the bicycle wheel, people won't likely say, "You have a few spokes that need attention and tuning," when they experience a ride on your bicycle. They are more likely to generalize and say, "Your bike stinks." In the same way, people can make sweeping judgments about authenticity and genuineness based on small cues and data. To lead with authenticity, effective managers develop new behaviors and find appropriate ways to work with the structural and the people sides of change. They don't swing wildly from one end to the other. By learning about the twelve change-related leadership competencies described in the following chapters and how they relate to each other, managers and executives can tease out adjustments to maintain or improve their level of trust and effectiveness as situations change.

Understanding the Competencies

Each of the following chapters addresses a pair of competencies, showing what each competency looks like when it is overdone and underdone, and what the right balance between the two looks like. Each chapter also provides some guidelines that managers can use to develop each competency, and a simple way to gauge which competencies they need to emphasize during extraordinary times. We begin with an overview of the twelve competencies:

Catalyzing change is championing an initiative or significant change. A leader who is skilled at catalyzing change consistently promotes the cause, encourages others to get on board, and reinforces those who already are. Such leaders are highly driven and eager to get others engaged in new initiatives.

Coping with transition involves recognizing and addressing the personal and emotional elements of change. Leaders who are able to cope with transition are in touch with their personal reactions to change and transition and make use of that emotional information. They lead by example.

Sense of urgency involves taking action quickly when necessary to keep things rolling. Leaders who have a strong sense of urgency move fast on issues and accelerate the pace for everyone. They value action and know how to get things done.

Realistic patience involves knowing when and how to slow the pace to allow time and space for people to cope and adapt. Leaders who display realistic patience appreciate the fact that people learn and deal with change differently and do not judge them based on their own styles, preferences, or capabilities.

Being tough denotes the ability to make difficult decisions about issues and people with little hesitation or second-guessing. Leaders who are comfortable and secure with themselves can display toughness; they're not afraid to take a stand in the face of public opinion or strong resistance.

Being empathetic requires taking others' perspectives into account when making decisions and taking action. Empathetic leaders try to put themselves in other people's shoes; they're able to enhance their own perspectives by considering the views of others.

Optimism is the ability to see the positive potential of any challenge. Leaders who exude optimism can communicate and convey that optimism to others.

The combination of *realism and openness* denotes a grounded perspective and a willingness to be candid. Leaders who practice this competency are clear and honest about assessing a situation and the prospects for the future. They are candid in communicating what is known and not known. When managers exhibit realism and openness, they speak the truth, don't sugarcoat the facts, and are willing to admit personal mistakes and foibles.

Self-reliance involves a willingness to take a lead role and even to do something yourself when necessary. Self-reliant leaders have a great deal of confidence in their skills and abilities and are willing to step up and tackle new challenges.

Trusting others means being comfortable with allowing others to do their part of a task or project. A leader who trusts others is open to input and support from colleagues and friends. Such leaders respect others and demonstrate trust through a willingness to be vulnerable with them.

Capitalizing on strengths entails knowing your strengths and attributes, and confidently applying them to tackle new situations and circumstances. A leader who knows how to capitalize on strengths trusts the abilities that have generated success, rewards, recognition, compliments, and promotions in the past and uses them in new situations.

Going against the grain entails a willingness to learn and try new things, even when the process is hard or painful. Leaders who can go against the grain are willing to get out of their comfort zones. They are willing to tolerate discomfort if it leads to learning.

You may have noticed in reading these brief descriptions that each of these capabilities is important; at the same time there are some inherent conflicts between and paradoxes among them. That's because in the face of change and turmoil, people look for leaders who are simultaneously strong and vulnerable, heroic and open, demanding and compassionate. Managing well amid those opposing demands can feel like an impossible balancing act. Finding the right behaviors, tone, and style to lead effectively during times of change is largely about blending characteristics that appear paradoxical, but that coexist as a measure of a leader's authenticity.

Managing the dynamic tension between opposing competencies—using more of one than the other, or some of both, and being able to move between them with some flexibility and grace—is not easy. The point of stability can be different for different situations and at different points in time (describing all the possibilities is well beyond the scope of this book). Appropriately balancing these twelve competencies is a subtle and fragile process, and it becomes even more so during times of stress. If you develop your facility for a range of behaviors and learn to spot signs that your leadership is out of true, you will be better prepared to lead in times of upheaval and transition. Over time, leaders and their organizations do better if leaders develop an agile resilience, know when it's necessary to move between opposing competencies, and are able to do so.

Let's return to the stories of our managers—Rachel, Antonio, and Mitchell—and examine their patterns of leadership behavior to better understand the dynamics of the twelve competencies.

Rachel, the Fortune 50 division vice president, does not have the trust of her employees, and the board of directors is beginning to lose confidence in her. What has happened?

If you look at Rachel's leadership style as it's plotted on the wheel on the next page, you'll see that she significantly emphasizes the structural elements of leadership. The people side of her wheel suffers from her neglect. Convinced she is in the right, Rachel may not realize that her personal frustration and desire to make the change happen are playing out in perceptions that she is condescending, insensitive, and aggressive. Her direct reports say, "She just won't listen." She seems oblivious to the depth of her group's concerns and becomes defensive when someone tries to bring them to her attention. With such a focus on structural issues, it's clear to others—but not so clear to Rachel—why she hasn't been able to harness the support, energy, and talent of the people around her. Her direct reports have become conditioned not to speak honestly to her. In their words, "It's just not safe."

RACHEL'S WHEEL

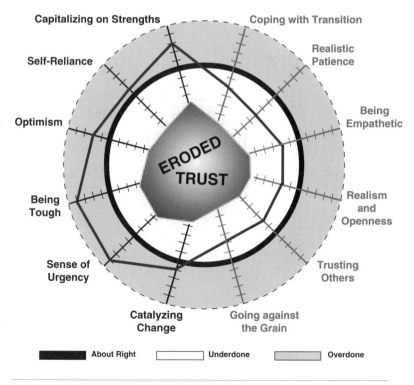

Antonio is struggling with his transition because of a different combination of overdoing and underdoing. When his leadership style is plotted on the wheel below, it's clear that Antonio's experience with the people side of leadership is certainly better developed than Rachel's. However, he tries to shoulder the burden of change by himself, determined to stick with the plan and champion change. Under stress, his behavior becomes more extreme on several of the dimensions, creating confusion among the people with whom he works. He thinks he is protecting his people, but in reality they feel unsupported and frustrated. The organization feels that Antonio is losing his edge. He isn't implementing his changes and appears not

ANTONIO'S WHEEL

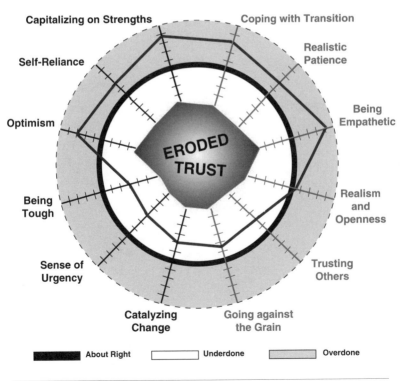

to be holding others accountable. The plan is in danger of falling apart.

Mitchell, in contrast to Rachel and Antonio, is leading himself and others through transition in a balanced, effective way. His wheel, below, is not a perfect circle, but neither is leadership really a bicycle wheel. Maintaining the right balance among the twelve competencies doesn't mean that Mitchell gives every dimension equal emphasis or that he calculates every word and action. Rather, it indicates that Mitchell has accurately assessed both the business climate and the emotional climate in which he works. He is astute in his political and relational roles and has a good handle on his own emotional

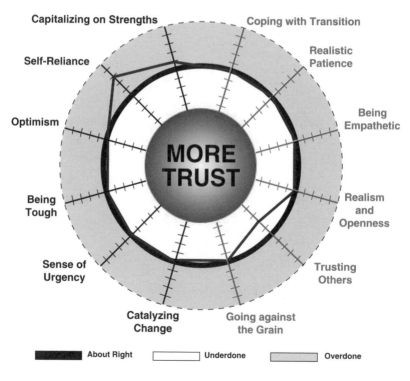

MITCHELL'S WHEEL

reality. Mitchell is able to blend his skills and adapt his approach. Even though his work situation is stressful, he feels authentic, true to himself. His direct reports and others react to his authenticity and see him as an effective leader.

Perhaps the biggest challenge you will face in practicing an authentic brand of leadership is finding the right point of dynamic balance in those areas where your own assumptions about leadership lead you to emphasize one set of competencies over another, particularly in times of stress. These tendencies have their origins in your personality traits, your education, your training, and your lifelong learning experiences. Reaching the right point of balance doesn't require emphasizing each competency to the same degree. You may find, for example, that a slight increase in your empathy or your openness toward others goes a long way toward resolving the concerns people have over a new process or system. Or you may find that your being more direct and more willing to make hard decisions can provide the clarity and confidence people seek in an ambiguous situation.

Generally, the key to leading with authenticity in extraordinary times is to neither exaggerate nor downplay any of the twelve competencies. However, highly effective leaders can and do intentionally overplay one or two elements to great effect. This tactic works when two things hold true: First, the leader chooses a behavior and is not reacting defensively. Second, the leader astutely pulls closer to true over time. This attention to the situation at hand and the agility required to shift emphasis from one competency to its opposite are hallmarks of a leader whom people trust to lead change.

2

CATALYZING CHANGE VERSUS COPING WITH TRANSITION

Striking a balance between catalyzing change and coping with transition helps you establish your authenticity and trustworthiness as a leader. Catalyzing change involves the ability to manage an initiative or change, generate acceptance and support, and see things through. Coping with transition involves the ability to recognize and address the personal and emotional fallout that accompanies change.

Leaders who are skilled at catalyzing change consistently promote the cause, encourage others to get on board, and reinforce those who already are. They are highly driven and are eager to get others engaged in any new initiative. Leaders who are able to understand and cope with transitions are in touch with their personal reactions to change and are comfortable sharing those emotions. They walk the talk and lead by example. A leader who is adept at both catalyzing the change and coping with the complexities of transition creates a climate and culture for working through difficult times. Trust and commitment are maintained at a higher level, and the transition ultimately gains momentum as people work through the process.

The fast pace and complex challenges that typify today's organizations push most leaders to focus on catalyzing change at the expense of helping people deal with the transition during the change. Typically, top leaders have well-developed strategies and plans, roll them out, utilize a range of communication tactics, and are then ready to move on with the implementation. Often they wonder why a change initiative is faltering, why a new system isn't showing the anticipated return, or why people aren't moving on and getting with the program.

When a leader overdoes catalyzing change and minimizes coping with transition, he or she is likely to have unrealistic expectations. Typically, such a leader sets up a high-pressure environment and underestimates the negative impact the change and the pressure may have on others. Always putting a positive spin on change, this leader is often perceived as speaking idly, misleadingly, boastfully. Exaggerated attempts at reassurance end up being perceived as phony and condescending. This results in a number of negative individual and organizational consequences. A leader can easily lose credibility and be viewed as false and insincere. People in the organization become disillusioned and disconnected.

Of course, the opposite set of overdoing and underdoing has its own perils. By overemphasizing the process of coping with transition, a leader can easily run a change effort into the ground. If the leader doesn't have sufficient ability to catalyze change, the direction becomes unclear and people lose energy and enthusiasm. The organization and individuals can become stuck and over-whelmed. Emotional reactions run the gamut and are likely to include frustration, anger, resistance, and depression.

When leaders balance catalyzing change and coping with transition, the way in which others perceive their behavior is based on two elements: what they say and what they do.

1. Leaders need to communicate effectively by sharing their thinking and the story behind their reasoning—not just the final decision or strategy. During times of change, leaders want people to grasp the importance of the changes, and they hope that people will agree with the rationale and the process. On the other hand, people want a clear understanding of the background strategy—why the change? Part of the inherent challenge of leading people in extraordinary times is that they are often skeptical. As a

result, they have a thirst for information. The level of understanding and agreement the leader stimulates can affect the degree of enthusiasm people bring to their individual roles in the change.

2. Along with a rationale, people need reassurance. While the leader's role involves convincing others to get on board for a change initiative, bombarding them with information has limitations. A critical component of leading change is to model the behavior and demonstrate the resilience that will take people through the transition. People need to see leaders living and integrating the changes that they advocate. If they don't see that, they can become skeptical and even resistant. If a leader is inconsistent—saying one thing but doing another—doubt and resistance arise, damaging integrity and eroding trust.

One of the best CEOs we've worked with excels at both driving change and coping with the complexities of transition. Jay runs an enormous, sprawling organization with a long history and an entrenched bureaucracy. Yet he is challenging the organization to be a different and more competitive business. As a true visionary leader, Jay is thinking way ahead of everyone else in the organization. He champions new ideas, new strategies, and new ways of working with clarity, passion, and intensity. But alongside his push for change, Jay respects the organization's roots and is committed to helping his people cope with the fallout of the change. Always honest and direct, he readily talks about the emotional and practical difficulties employees face, given the pressure to change. Over and over again, he makes the case for change. He lays out the imperative and then says, "I know it's not easy, but we're going to help you. Here are some things that will help us work through it." Jay also adds his own authentic experience with change and transition, telling his own stories and giving examples and encouragement. Jay has invested in leader development programs and formal mechanisms to acknowledge and facilitate transition, but most important, he models the behavior he is asking of his people.

Leaders who are skilled at catalyzing change

- ❏ understand the rationale for a shift in direction
- ❏ communicate the vision with enthusiasm and energy
- ❏ demonstrate how the change is a win for the organization and its people
- ❏ engage those who are resistant
- ❏ make themselves accessible for formal and informal discussions
- ❏ talk the talk and walk the walk
- ❏ listen to understand other points of view
- ❏ marshal the resources to drive the change
- ❏ speak truth to power when necessary

Leaders who cope well with transition

- ❏ are in touch with their own reactions and feelings about the change
- ❏ understand the difference between change and transition
- ❏ give themselves and others permission to experience and express loss and grieving

- model vulnerability so that others are able to move through transition stages
- are realistic about the challenges people can handle
- communicate with staff at all levels
- tell people as much as they can about the situation
- push back on senior management when appropriate
- celebrate successes along the way

Making It True

Where do you begin? What steps can you take to strike a balance between catalyzing change and coping with transition?

Communicate. Effective leaders are relentless communicators. Find many ways to share information and keep processes open and transparent. Talk about your thoughts and feelings. Good communicators are also good listeners, so pay attention both to what is said and to what is not said.

Don't dismiss the old. Ignoring, demeaning, or dismissing the way things used to be prevents people from moving through the transition process. Help people through transition by acknowledging their history and attachments. The new is built on the old. There will be many opportunities to apply past lessons to new challenges.

Make yourself more visible. If you communicate well, you won't be out of sight. But be sure to be visible and accessible as much as possible; people can't be influenced by behavior they don't see. You must find ways to interact with all of your stakeholder groups. Although this seems fairly obvious, there are several reasons why executives are less visible during rough times. The obvious and legitimate reason is that you have little extra time. But it also may be that you are uncomfortable or worn out from facing employees who feel threatened and defensive. While you may prefer to avoid putting yourself out there as a target for negative feedback, it is essential to do so in order to effectively lead others through transition.

Be genuine. This involves making more of yourself available. Let people see who you are. What kind of person are you in times of stress, crisis, and change? This involves taking off the masks or armor you have put on over the years and being real with people. Others want to know that you are genuine in what you say, feel, and do before they invest their trust in you. What's more, people under stress have a heightened sensitivity for assessing who is being genuine and who isn't. This means it is more important to be yourself than to act like an executive. You will probably feel somewhat vulnerable and uncomfortable, but masking rarely fools people and your self-protective efforts will only serve to erode your trustworthiness.

Reinforce authenticity. Learn to recognize and reinforce authentic, resilient behavior patterns in others. Keep your antenna up to spot the kind of behavior that can build an open community with high integrity. You will send a signal that these genuine behaviors are noticed and rewarded. This will help spread your good intention throughout the organization.

Find inspiration. You need your own touchstones or reminders about what you are trying to accomplish, what your problems are, and how you want to behave. Adopt a quote, parable, cliché, picture, or other symbol to help you stay connected to your situation. Examples include the following: Walk the talk. Practice what you preach. Trust is earned by the penny and spent by the dollar. What you do is so loud, I can't hear what you're saying.

	Overdone	Underdone
Catalyzing Change	• Applies top-down pressure • Puts spin on change • Ignores negative impact on self and others • Hides own vulnerability • Appears to be in denial of unintended consequences • Has unrealistic expectations	• Doesn't champion change • Doesn't get the message out • Fosters doubt in others • Fails to create energy and focus • Undermines credibility • Inhibits the process
Coping with Transition	• Is too focused on self • May be overwhelmed • Second-guesses change • Fails to implement change • Creates new barriers	• Wears emotional mask • Ignores others' emotions • Attempts to "suck it up" • Stays detached • Is an unhealthy role model • Is awkward or insincere in understanding others

3
SENSE OF URGENCY VERSUS REALISTIC PATIENCE

One of the most critical responsibilities of a transition leader involves maintaining energy, momentum, and productivity in the face of change. Having a sense of urgency or a need to "get on with it" is an important element of the revitalization process for the leaders and for other members of the group. In addition, leaders are likely to receive pressure from above to hurry up and get people moving toward the desired outcomes. The skills associated with a sense of urgency allow leaders to be action oriented and keep things rolling. Leaders who have a strong sense of urgency move on issues quickly and motivate others to work at a rapid pace, stay focused, and get results. They value action and know how to get things done.

Equally important but rarely addressed in times of change is the importance of having enough patience with the transition process. Realistic patience involves knowing when and how to slow the pace to allow time and space for people to cope and adapt. This means recognizing that people need differing amounts of time and effort to understand and adapt to change. As in any grief or loss experience, there is a natural cycle to the process of letting go of the old and connecting with the new. Leaders must learn how to honor this cycle in others if the transition effort is to be successful in the long term. Failure to have patience with people can actually increase their resistance, and thereby hinder their process of adapting.

Leaders who overdo sense of urgency and downplay realistic patience are too insistent, too quick to announce changes, and too eager to take action. They fail to prioritize, making everything equally urgent. This fosters resistance and even fear. Often, in a rush to make their marks, these leaders instead erode their credibility and stymie the energy, motivation, and creativity of the very people they need on board to make their initiatives successful.

When managers do the opposite—when they overdo realistic patience and downplay sense of urgency—everything is a work in progress, deadlines are extended, and employees wonder whether the planned changes will ever take place. In an attempt to protect themselves or others, these leaders seem to hold off the change. But rather than appreciating the "protection," people are more likely to feel that such leaders are causing more stress by putting off the inevitable and not making firm decisions. This indecisive and un-inspiring leadership also frustrates those who are ready to move on.

So what does it look like when a leader addresses both sense of urgency and realistic patience? How does managing this pair of competencies help establish a team that is committed, trustworthy, and loyal? Leaders who balance sense of urgency and realistic patience focus on four key actions:

1. They articulate expectations. Clearly explaining why, how, and when things need to happen sets up expectations and creates a healthy level of stress and pressure. It also establishes a mechanism for monitoring and addressing performance.

2. They accurately gauge pace. When such leaders say something is urgent, it really is. They don't panic, overreact, or make everything equally urgent or important. They are able to prioritize. They recognize when to slow down in order to speed up later.

3. They give support through the struggle. Helping the team get on with it without driving them past the point of productivity gives people a chance to keep up when they

are struggling. These leaders make a conscious effort to provide extra support and guidance when appropriate. They give people feedback so they know whether they're getting it or not. They foster credibility by achieving a balance between urgency and compassion.

4. They demonstrate flexible control. Leaders who set the right tone between control and flexibility are respected and viewed as competent—as well as caring and in touch with employees.

We worked recently with a company in an intense turnaround mode. They brought in Tom, an executive known for his decisive style, for an important "fix-it" assignment. Right away he dismissed a lot of the staff that he had inherited, quickly making the decision that they were much of the problem. Priding himself on his ability to be decisive, he pushed action and made swift change. Unfortunately, his decisions were not sufficiently thought out, and he gained a reputation for making quick but unwise decisions. His shoot-from-the-hip style cut out a lot of good people, alienated others, and led to mistakes that could have been prevented.

Ironically, those looking down from above initially thought Tom was just what the doctor ordered. His approach was applauded and rewarded by top management. He was characterized as a take-charge executive who was willing to make the tough calls on both issues and people. It was only when things began to unravel in a morass of tactical errors and deflated morale that his transition leadership skills were called into question and he was reassigned.

IN BALANCE

Sense of
Urgency ━━━━━━━ **TRUST** ━━━━━━━ Realistic
Patience

Leaders who demonstrate a healthy sense of urgency

- ❏ create clear expectations and timelines
- ❏ explain why the urgency
- ❏ provide data to support the urgency
- ❏ set and adjust priorities
- ❏ provide resources and clear obstacles
- ❏ remind about deadlines
- ❏ encourage more than berate
- ❏ articulate the "now" and the vision
- ❏ walk the talk
- ❏ make timely decisions
- ❏ create healthy level of stress and pressure
- ❏ monitor the team's ability to deliver

Leaders who exhibit realistic patience

- ❏ explain the why and how of what needs to be done
- ❏ coach people who are struggling
- ❏ are patient with the emotional realities—their own and those of their followers
- ❏ understand that performance may initially lag
- ❏ set interim targets for people
- ❏ put things into different words or contexts to help bring people along
- ❏ don't stay patient forever—but give people space and time to learn and cope
- ❏ set a range of outcomes so people have a chance to be successful

Making It True

What steps can you take to strike the right chord when it comes to demonstrating both a sense of urgency and realistic patience? Here are some guidelines:

Meet them where they are. If you want to lead people somewhere new, you need to understand where they are. What have they experienced in the past? What have they been told before? What is completely new? What do they value? What do they fear they are losing? What do they have personally at stake? Remember that your role in the leadership process probably puts you in a position of having more input, more control, more information, and earlier warnings than those who are looking to you for guidance. In those moments when you are frustrated by the hesitancy and reluctance of people to change, remember that, unlike you, they are probably just learning about some of the changes for the first time. It will require patience on your part to allow people the time and space to go through the natural stages of letting go before they will be ready to catch up with you. Try as you might, you can't shake people hard enough to put them on your timetable for acceptance and recovery.

Prioritize and pace. Be sure to set and honor priorities. Arrange activities and events in a way that will build to the new reality in stages. While there is always much to do, every event cannot be urgent and every task cannot be a number one priority. Change and transition are demanding experiences that can exhaust the most committed of employees. Set stretch targets that are achievable. Whenever possible, create interim milestones that will allow people to achieve success along the way.

Take time to listen. Allow people to air their gripes and complaints. Some of what you will hear grows out of the pain of having to learn new methods and strategies. On the other hand, some of it may reflect valid evaluations of the gaps and discontinuities in the evolving design. In either case, it is important to allow people the time and space to vent their concerns and voice their alternative strategies—even if nothing can be done to alter the overall plans.

Avoid swift judgment. Don't dismiss, write off, or label employees too easily or too quickly. People differ in ways that can affect their degree of readiness and rate of response to transition. These may include personality, experience, situations outside work, and organizational expectations. Remember that the initial stages of the normal transition response pattern include denial, withdrawal, and frustration. Even a more evolved reaction will often include various forms of resistance, anger, and rejection. Displaying the patience that encourages people to work their way to a healthier commitment can pay huge dividends in the end.

Don't squash resistance. Establish a climate that processes resistance rather than attempting to squash it. Generally there is useful information in the way people resist change and transition. All change involves loss. The nature of resistance can inform you about what people value and what they are afraid of losing. At a minimum, that sense of loss needs to be acknowledged. Perhaps more important, there may be embedded information about aspects of the environment that should not be swept aside or lost in the course of change. There may be wisdom in maintaining some things as they were.

Coach, teach, and model. Spend some of your time and energy in coaching, teaching, and modeling the adaptive process for others. If you can honor the past and model the present and future, you will encourage others by your example.

	Overdone	Underdone
Sense of Urgency	• Insists, pressures • Runs ahead of plan • Makes everything a priority • Is impersonal • Blocks resistance • Pushes too hard	• Doesn't commit to change • Yields to resistance • Is reluctant to push others • Is indecisive and uninspiring • Conflicts with culture • Moves too slowly
Realistic Patience	• Can be manipulated • Fails to implement • Doesn't inspire others • Frustrates those who are ready to move on • Is soft on people issues	• Doesn't listen well • Won't acknowledge loss • Hides own feelings • Gives up on people • Generates fear • Fosters resistance

4

BEING TOUGH VERSUS BEING EMPATHETIC

A leader must be tough enough to make difficult, bottom-line decisions that serve the overall needs of the organization. Being tough involves being decisive and unafraid to take a stand in the face of public opinion or strong resistance. And you must also make such decisions with sensitivity to the impact and consequences for others in the organization. Failure to do so can erode loyalty and trust, as well as morale and motivation—at the very time when you need them most.

On the other hand, the ability to be empathetic encourages loyalty and trust—even understanding of and support for difficult decisions. Being empathetic involves taking others' perspectives into account when making decisions and taking action. It means being able to accurately anticipate or at least recognize the emotional impact of decisions and actions. Empathetic leaders are able to put themselves in other people's shoes, consider individual limitations, set aside preconceived notions, and value people as well as results. The ability to be empathetic is also grounded in self-awareness; it's hard to be empathetic if you are not in touch with your own emotions and reactions.

This dimension is one that is incredibly difficult for many leaders to get right. Often they have been taught to shut down their emotional connections or empathy in order to make the difficult decisions. They worry that if they let their soft side show, it will be viewed as weakness or as a lack of commitment to the decisions. Our experience in working with leaders has shown the exact opposite to be true in times of significant change and crisis. People want to know that their leaders can be tough, committed, and decisive, but they want them to be human—and humane—too.

Overdoing toughness while underdoing empathy creates fairly obvious and, unfortunately, common results. The relentless drive for results buries concerns for people, and the leader appears inhuman and uncaring. An environment of alienation and fear is created. Learning is stifled because people are afraid to take risks or make mistakes, and the voices of contrary data and opinion are silenced. People lose commitment and focus, so results are often lost as well.

On the flip side, underdoing toughness while overdoing empathy hinders change and is a huge disservice to people and the organization. Both the leader and the company are perceived to be soft and wishy-washy. When the leader lacks firmness and pressure, results are viewed as less important, and the group can become directionless. This also creates a climate where manipulation, favoritism, and power struggles can dominate.

When leaders temper toughness with genuine empathy, the vision and direction are clear. Targets, goals, and expectations seem high, but attainable. People know how to get where they're going. Individuals feel valued and heard, and leaders are viewed as genuine. This happens because such leaders are equally comfortable in addressing two apparently paradoxical needs:

1. They don't shy away from difficulty. Leaders who strike a balance between toughness and empathy hold themselves as well as others accountable, even in challenging situations. Demonstrating perseverance, they accept difficulty but do not use it as an excuse or crutch. Challenge is faced directly, with a close eye on results.

2. They pay attention to emotions. While driving for results and change, these leaders listen carefully with an honest intent to understand. They recognize and respond to the

emotional impact their demands and decisions are causing. They stay connected to their own emotional reactions to the organization and its situation so that they can authentically communicate with and relate to others.

We worked closely with one CEO whose company was knee-deep in downsizing. Ian had been with the organization for more than thirty years and was closely connected to the employees and the community. By the time the company got to the third round of downsizing, however, he had completely detached from people. We encouraged him to reconnect and show his human side, but he kept saying, "I'm driving the change, and if I let my guard down, it will all fall apart." He called us one day and said, "I blew it. I was making the announcement of the next round of layoffs, and I lost control." Here's what happened.

At a company meeting, he was reading his carefully prepared statement (approved by the legal and HR departments) about how many people would be cut, what resources would be available, what the buyout package would be, and so forth. Right in the middle of it, he stopped. He took off his glasses, looked out at his people, teared up, and said, "Sometimes you must think that I'm horrible and that I don't have any feelings. This is so hard for me to do. I grew up in this business. Some of the people that are leaving, I worked for them on the way up. Some of them shaped me as a leader; some are my friends. I understand why they don't fit anymore, and I understand why they are leaving, but it just breaks my heart. These are good people. This is really hard. It's really hard for them, and it's really hard for me too." Then he put his glasses back on, took a deep breath, and read the rest of the statement.

Ian thought it was terrible that he had lost control. In follow-up meetings and through interactions with others in the organization, we found that this forty-five-second interlude was, in fact, a positive and powerful event. To his astonishment, Ian learned that the ripples that went across the company were ones of support and recognition: "That's the guy I know . . . the guy I used to work for . . . I knew that he cared about us . . . he was probably trying to be strong for the company." The difficult decisions did not change, but people were relieved and reassured because the CEO had shown his own vulnerability. He demonstrated that he also struggled with the difficulty of the situation and in doing so allowed people to reconnect with him.

This is not to say, however, that everyone should lose control or tear up to show empathy. This CEO's behavior was authentic; he took a mask off and was himself. To demonstrate empathy, leaders can pay close attention to their own emotions and show their emotions and empathy in a way that is real. But don't fake compassion or stage your authenticity. It will backfire.

IN BALANCE

Being Tough — TRUST — Being Empathetic

Leaders who demonstrate a good level of toughness

❏ hold themselves and others accountable
❏ set clear goals and expectations for performance
❏ challenge people to adopt an attitude of continuous improvement

- display perseverance through adversity
- are firm and assertive, but fair and evenhanded
- maintain focus and alignment with corporate goals
- identify, prioritize, and measure key activities
- don't tolerate nonsense, but operate in a reasonable manner
- can be demanding and tough without being a bully

Leaders who demonstrate a good sense of empathy

- listen with an honest intent to understand
- set aside preconceived notions
- value people as well as results
- give honest and direct feedback in a genuine manner
- are kind but not soft
- make allowances for difficult situations
- value diversity and appreciate different perspectives
- understand the emotional impact of demands
- consider individual limitations and barriers
- communicate openly
- use analogies and stories to make points

Making It True

To strike a balance between being tough and being empathetic, consider the following guidelines:

Define *toughness* and *empathy* for yourself. Where is the toughness line for you? Make a list of escalating indicators of being tough. Start with behaviors that you would consider a little tough (such as requiring a meeting with someone), and then add descriptors of increasingly tough behaviors. Add items all the way to behaviors that are well beyond what would be an acceptable level of toughness for you (such as expressing your dissatisfaction physically). Once you have drafted your list, draw a line indicating the line you would not wish to cross in being tough with people. How broad is your range? What might your boss or direct reports say about where you drew your line? Is it appropriate? Accurate? Honest? Repeat the above exercise for empathy. Where would you draw your empathy line?

Pay attention to unintended consequences. Always ask, "What are the unintended consequences of this decision?" It is good practice to consider as many consequences as possible. These consequences have to be weighed against the positive long-term impact of the decision at hand. Invariably you are forced to consider trade-offs. Dilemmas reign supreme during transitions because no single answer can satisfy all of the complexities of organizational problems. Exploring the less obvious consequences will at least allow you to make informed choices that will be better understood by the affected stakeholders.

Reassess trade-offs. Review your decisions from time to time to see whether the trade-offs continue to make sense. Do your original assumptions still hold true? Have there been consequences or trade-offs that you didn't anticipate? Are you responding and making decisions based on fixed patterns or habits? Take time to reflect on your actions or, better yet, to seek input from others so that you can prevent overdoing toughness or empathy.

Customize your approach. Think of a few people who look to you for leadership. How do you balance toughness (challenge) with empathy (support) for each of them? Are you taking individual differences into account? Do you use a one-size-fits-all approach regardless of individual needs? Beyond self-reflection, consider what others might say in private about your philosophy of applying toughness and empathy. Or take the extra step and solicit real feedback from others you trust.

Don't shun challenging issues or avoid conflict. By avoiding the difficult people or difficult issues, you can do great harm to yourself, your coworkers, and your organization. As a leader, you are obligated to be tough enough to deal with challenge and conflict.

Get comfortable in the hot seat. As a leader you will bear the brunt of many people's anger, frustration, and confusion. You will be scrutinized. Not everyone will interpret your behavior as you intend it. People will notice any inconsistency between your talk and walk. Both your behavior and your words might be reported out of context. Accept that this is part of a leader's life.

Don't overpersonalize business. While empathizing with others allows you to guide them through transition, it can also be overdone if you personalize your work relationships. You cannot be responsible for taking care of everyone, nor can you ensure that everyone will be successful.

	Overdone	Underdone
Being Tough	• Is aggressive, pressures • Bullies others • Is insensitive, alienates • Treats people coldly • Denies own vulnerability • Labels and punishes	• Shuns challenging issues • Doesn't deliver results • Is too soft in moving others • Avoids conflict • Is a sucker for excuses • Is wishy-washy, spineless • Lacks accountability
Being Empathetic	• Is too sensitive to emotions • Allows people to flounder • Personalizes business at an unhealthy level • Plays favorites • May appear phony and unreliable	• Is cold, abrupt, insensitive • Doesn't understand • Is self-centered, uncaring • Keeps people at a distance • Is not approachable • Has to have his or her own way

5
OPTIMISM VERSUS REALISM AND OPENNESS

Leaders have a key role to play in maintaining hope and commitment in the face of transition. When people are stressed by a crisis or major upheaval, they look to their leaders for positive energy and confidence. Optimism is the ability to see the positive potential of any challenge. A leader who exudes optimism is a "glass is half full" kind of person who communicates and conveys that optimism to others.

But optimism must not be blind or ungrounded. It should be balanced with and validated by realism and openness. This means having a grounded perspective and a willingness to be candid. Leaders who are realistic are clear and honest about assessing a situation and prospects for the future. They are candid and open in communicating what is known and not known. When managers exhibit realism and openness, they speak the truth, don't sugarcoat the facts, and are willing to admit personal mistakes and foibles. Credibility is essential for leading through change and transition. When leaders fail to be honest and candid, trust and credibility are damaged.

Sometimes, managers overdo the optimism side in an effort to encourage others to make the transition. When overdoing optimism and underdoing openness, they are usually thinking, "I'm supposed to buy in, inspire people to do this work. I'm supposed to be optimistic. My people can't know that I have my own doubts, concerns, and unanswered questions." This behavior, however, may create a false sense of reality that can lead to complacency. Most people can tell when a leader is overdoing optimism. They view this as naïveté at best and deception at worst. Opposing or more realistic opinions are blocked and can lead to poor decision making. Overdoing optimism erodes trust in the leader and deflates the motivation and energy of employees.

However, underdoing optimism and overdoing openness can also erode trust and shut down progress. The leader sets up a situation of too much talk and not enough direction and action. The leader plants doubt and dilutes hope. Either the leader or the group may become paralyzed by inaction and fear of making mistakes. Loss of confidence in the leader adds to the confusion of change and transition, as well as disloyalty, indecisiveness, and untrustworthiness.

A leader who effectively blends optimism with realism and openness exudes honesty and integrity. People in the organization are energized by a clear vision that takes into account current reality. People trust the leader not to ignore problem areas or try to mislead them. Rather, the leader is optimistic even with a clear understanding of the difficulties involved. Because of this, group members feel confident in both the leader and themselves to address what's coming. Leaders who are both optimistic and realistic display two important characteristics:

1. They are genuinely committed to the change, strategy, or initiative. True optimism comes from belief in the purpose or direction of change. The authentic leader is committed to the fundamental approach for achieving goals, yet is able to adapt and improvise in order to get there.

2. They aren't afraid of truth. A commitment to genuine change requires honesty and clarity. An effective leader won't shy away from reality. In fact, such leaders will ask the hard questions and foster an environment of honesty and candid discussion.

One vice president we know hits the mark on balancing optimism with realism. Prior to joining her company, Christine had been an analyst for the industry. Her ability to clearly read a situation for what it is has enabled her to bring a steady, predictable encouragement to the company's major strategic shift. She is completely behind the new direction and is a primary supporter and motivator in the organization. Yet she knows the details (both good and bad) and is honest about individual and organizational struggles. Her colleagues and direct reports told us: "From day to day she doesn't waver with her optimism or diminish her support as we go through the ups and downs . . . very stable . . . she'll deal with the realities of where we are."

IN BALANCE

Optimism ████████ **TRUST** ████████ Realism and Openness

Leaders who demonstrate a good level of optimism

- ❏ offer hopeful projections of the future
- ❏ generate a contagious level of energy, enthusiasm, and optimism
- ❏ are creative and thoughtful about the challenges of the change process
- ❏ create and communicate a clear vision
- ❏ push themselves and others to set and strive for stretch targets
- ❏ consistently walk the talk
- ❏ authentically present the range of possible strategies and risks
- ❏ offer engaging ideas and plans
- ❏ know what others need to be successful

Leaders who demonstrate a good sense of realism and openness

❏ make others comfortable by sharing of self
❏ have open channels of communication
❏ trust the team to be capable of handling the truth
❏ are honest and engaging in discussions
❏ acknowledge setbacks and mistakes
❏ don't try to mask real problems
❏ use candor to engender trust and respect
❏ recogize barriers and limitations, and don't try to hide them
❏ share and empathize in a genuine way

Making It True

Here are ways to learn to balance optimism with realism and openness:

Show your enthusiasm. Energy and optimism are contagious. Rather than telling people that they should be positive and optimistic about the future, strive to be open and visible in modeling grounded optimism for them. Being optimistic speaks more powerfully than setting policy, making pronouncements, or cheerleading. If you are honest and sincere in your commitment to the future, people will read it on your face and observe it in your approach. But you can't fake it. If you aren't truly committed to where you are going, people will most likely see that as well.

Don't blow smoke. Avoid putting a false positive spin on decisions or events that are inherently negative or difficult to handle. People will see through these attempts and add personal resentment to the dislike they may already be feeling about the transition process.

Seek to understand obstacles and to learn from other perspectives. Don't overdo optimism and self-confidence to the point of not recognizing genuine barriers, obstacles, limitations, or mistakes. Use candor and honesty as vehicles for cultivating a higher level of trust and respect. Sharing the truth often provides a springboard for generating creative strategies and renewed energy.

Maintain open channels of communication. It is essential that you know what is going on, but people may not readily tell you the truth or give you feedback. You have to set the tone and model the behavior that makes truth telling okay. Although your instinct may be to retreat with your trusted advisers, you need to make a conscious effort to stay visibly connected to a broader circle of people. Make it clear that you want employees to share their concerns as well as their constructive ideas with you.

Trust people to be capable of handling the truth. Tell them what you know and own up to what you don't know. Most people understand that difficult challenges don't come wrapped in simple solutions. They don't expect their leaders to be superhuman, emotionless, or infallible. Indeed, they will be skeptical and cynical if you wear a mask and try to pretend to be something that you are not. Fight the urge to play the hero.

Don't hide from your reactions. Don't try to bury or deny your own human reactions to ongoing events. Powerful transitions trigger real emotions and feelings of loss and grieving in all of us. People pay close attention to their leaders in such times and are looking for indications that their leaders are real people who are capable of having human emotions like their own. They also look to you for validation that these emotional reactions are normal and acceptable. While people cannot wallow in their discomfort, it is quite normal for them to start there. Sharing honestly and from the heart will allow the grieving process to proceed in a more predictable fashion that will facilitate organizational healing in the long term.

	Overdone	Underdone
Optimism	• Oversells positives • Blows smoke • Is naive and clueless • Spews the party line • Doesn't own shortcomings • Is not authentic or genuine	• Has low confidence in future • Doesn't energize others • Is bland and uninspiring • Has no vision or passion • Is more of a follower • Has low resilience
Realism and Openness	• Is overly pessimistic • Won't buck status quo • Shares too much information • Leaks or vents excessively • Tries too hard to be one of the gang • Doesn't energize change	• Is a faker and a showman • Doesn't see downside • Withholds information • Hides own feelings • Ignores others' concerns • Is detached, aloof, and condescending • Is afraid to be vulnerable

6
SELF-RELIANCE VERSUS TRUSTING OTHERS

Today's organizations demand a challenging combination of individual talent and collective ability and effort. Leaders must develop the right level of self-reliance along with appropriate trust in and reliance upon others.

Self-reliance involves a willingness to take a lead role and do something yourself when necessary. A leader who is self-reliant has a great deal of confidence in his or her own skills and abilities and is willing to step up and tackle most new challenges as they arise.

Trusting others involves being comfortable about allowing others to do their part of a task or project. A leader who trusts others is open to input and support from colleagues and friends. Such a leader respects others and demonstrates trust through a willingness to be vulnerable with them.

By overdoing self-reliance and underdoing trusting others, leaders shut down the interest, talent, and contribution of others. People are frustrated when they perceive that they are not needed or respected. Employees seek ways to change jobs, and talented employees elsewhere in the organization are reluctant to work for an overly self-reliant leader.

Eventually, the leader also suffers. If the job is going to get done, only one person can do it. Leaders who are overly self-reliant also tend to mask or bury their own emotions and not trust others to see their personal vulnerability. As a result, they don't get the support, empathy, and understanding they need. Ironically, this can cause them to "leak" their emotions in inappropriate ways.

Leaders who overemphasize trust in others run the risk of abdicating authority or leaving a group leaderless—struggling for direction, stability, and confidence. They tend to create a team or organization that lacks objectives and is reactive rather than proactive. This leader may wear others out with an excessive need for support, leaving others to feel that it is easier to go around them than to work through them. Equally damaging, this leader can be easily subjected to manipulation by more aggressive colleagues.

This pair of leadership competencies is among the most difficult to balance. Our historical image of leadership tends to reinforce the notion of the mythical heroic leader who is always strong, courageous, and self-reliant in the face of extraordinary challenges. The stereotypical male hero is often the strong, silent type with superhuman skills and a capacity to stand alone in the face of demands that might overwhelm mere mortals. In truth, however, leadership rises to new heights when a leader confronts the complexities and demands of the modern world with a team of strong and committed allies.

When a leader is able to combine self-reliance with trust in others, a win-win atmosphere is established. People believe they have meaningful work and understand that the important contributions they make will be valued. And the leader doesn't feel isolated and alone in tackling emotional and operational changes. People feel free to speak truth to power—providing input, guidance, support, and feedback. This collaborative, confident approach contributes to individual and organizational learning that would otherwise not occur.

When leaders effectively balance self-reliance and trusting others, they exhibit three crucial behaviors:

1. They demonstrate high confidence in individuals and their ability to deliver results. Leaders are able to genuinely place trust in others who have been encouraged and supported in their work and development. By ensuring that others are

given appropriately challenging assignments and opportunities, the authentic leader places trust in others and, in turn, can choose when to be self-reliant.

2. They take a team approach to handling difficult issues. The greater the complexity of a situation, the more important it is to draw on the expertise and perspectives of others. A senior-level leader, accustomed to being the "expert," often feels exposed and vulnerable in doing this at first, but the rewards are substantial.

3. They can step in without micromanaging or undermining. When a pattern of trust has been established, the authentic leader can judiciously step in and advise, adjust, and, if needed, override. This is different from constant micromanaging and undermining. It is, in fact, the appropriate use of the authority bestowed by position and experience.

When we met Fred, a senior vice president of an energy company, he was self-reliant in the extreme. A total perfectionist, very confident, and incredibly brilliant, he didn't trust anyone else to do the work. Fred led his company with the assumption that everything would be better if he could touch it all himself. Yet Fred was also a really nice guy. People liked him, and he generally had good relationships. The people who worked for him told us, "He's the smartest leader I've ever worked for; I've learned a lot from watching him do things." Then they would add, "He's driving me crazy. He never lets me do anything. He double-checks all my work. He edits everything for grammar before he reads for content." We heard numerous stories of how people would work on projects for months, only to have Fred redo the work or change the direction in fifteen minutes. He was so individually driven and self-reliant that he had no skill at developing others, leading teams, delegating and letting go, or giving other people visibility and opportunity.

When Fred was given this kind of feedback during a CCL program, he was so upset that he called home. He told his wife, "People say I overcontrol things, I don't let people make decisions, I'm a perfectionist, and I'm horrible to work for." Imagine his shock when his wife agreed with the feedback and said he was the same way at home!

But Fred was driven to do something about his problem. He is an excellent example of how even established leaders can change—but his story also illustrates how arduous the process of change can be.

Fred decided he would practice giving up some control at home. He decided to have his two teenage sons plan the family vacation without his input or approval. The boys were so accustomed to their father's managing everything that they were suspicious and fearful about making any plans. First, they went to their mom and said, "This is a trick, right? Dad would never let us do this. We're going to screw this up and be grounded forever." Even with their mom's go-ahead, they were so unsure of themselves that they put off making a decision. When Fred insisted that they needed to decide something, they said, "We don't want to go anywhere. We just want to stay home and spend time with you." Fred and his family didn't go anywhere on vacation that summer.

Connecting the experience with his kids to his leadership role at work, Fred realized how his overcontrolling, self-reliant style prevented his direct reports from becoming more skilled and gaining experience. He saw more clearly how his behavior was limiting and frustrating those around him. So, convinced that he had to do a better job of developing his people, Fred started with a commitment to quit editing and revising the memos and reports of his staff. Instead, he told them, he would give verbal feedback. After three months, we asked him how it was going. "It's awful. They're worse than I thought. I can't have anything to write with around me; I even have to unpack my pockets." While it was really hard for him not to step in and rewrite and redo his employees' work, six months later he said, "They're getting there. They're writing better and taking more ownership. And it's not such a struggle for me."

For Fred, not editing was the most tangible way for him to practice letting go of control. By not revising his employees' work, he was starting to trust people to handle projects on their own. And since they had relied on him for so long to do their work, they were learning to be accountable and thorough. In the process of giving verbal feedback, Fred was also better able to coach and guide as a leader and engage in team processes.

At the end of a year, Fred joined us at a conference. He told his story—how hard it was to trust other people but that doing so had caused his people to improve. Someone asked him, "After a year of doing this, do your people write as well as you do now?" He replied, "Get serious! We're not doing miracles here. It's just management development."

The point of balancing self-reliance with trusting others is not to turn Fred (or anyone else) into somebody he's not. But what he learned was that he was way out of balance—that he needed to trust other people more. Good people were leaving the organization because they didn't want to work for him. His inability to develop and retain good managers was, in turn, disabling him and getting in the way of his ambition to be CEO. With this recognition and commitment to change, he improved. His behavior did change. He understood the relationship between self-reliance and trust—and why it matters—and became much better at balancing it.

Fred went on to become CEO and worked diligently to implement what he had learned. Instead of constantly criticizing others for not living up to his standards, he began creating development systems to facilitate their learning. He also created a self-monitoring system to remind himself not to leap in and wrest control when situations failed to unfold immediately as he expected them to. He made a conscious effort to trust his talented team of executives to lead their respective areas while relying more on his guidance than his direct intervention. All of these initiatives represented significant going against the grain for Fred, and the risk of falling back on his old pattern of overdoing and underdoing was ever present—particularly when the stakes were high and the pressure was on. But all his hard work bore significant fruit! In a follow-up assessment six years later, Fred was characterized as a champion of growth and development. His organization was viewed as one of the premier places in North America for managers to enhance their careers through experience and learning opportunities. Turnover at the senior level had become virtually nonexistent.

In his heart of hearts Fred would still prefer to put his personal stamp on every significant activity in the organization. His hardwired characteristics haven't changed, but he has crafted a new set of behaviors and expectations by fine-tuning the dynamic tension between his towering strengths and the equally important spokes on the opposite side of the wheel.

IN BALANCE

Self-
Reliance

TRUST

Trusting
Others

Leaders who demonstrate a good measure of self-reliance

❑ have confidence in their abilities

❑ have strength and energy that comes from within

❑ don't require validation from others

❑ have a comfortable self-knowledge of both strengths and
weaknesses

❑ are secure enough to access others when needed

❑ influence others with personal knowledge and experience

❑ set direction and expectations

❑ are resourceful and creative

❑ are open to learning new things

❑ are effective at self-management and seizing opportunities

Leaders who demonstrate a good level of trust in others

❑ trust others to know them as total people

❑ stay open to input and support

❑ are comfortable knowing others' strengths and relying on them

❑ practice listening to understand

❑ have confidence in themselves and others

❑ communicate what is expected of others

❑ are empathetic and understanding

❑ know others' strengths and rely on them

❑ engage actively when delegating (not blind trust)

❑ support others in doing their work their way

Making It True

How can you practice both self-reliance and trusting others? Here are some guidelines:

Gain an accurate sense of self. The expression of true self-reliance is contingent upon knowing and owning your personal strengths, weaknesses, and vulnerabilities. You won't know when and how much to trust your own judgment unless you are working from a healthy base of self-awareness, self-understanding, and self-acceptance. Coming to terms with your own assets and liabilities will give you the courage to be more open in accepting the input of others. It will also help you identify areas where you might give others opportunities to contribute more in their strength areas.

Don't isolate yourself. Create an environment in which others feel safe to offer guidance, input, and support. The higher you go in leadership roles, the less likely people will be to offer suggestions, reactions, and feedback to you. This is particularly true if their input conflicts with opinions you have expressed publicly. It's part of your job to create the space for others to make meaningful contributions. They must know that you value and trust them.

Don't shoulder the burden alone. Being a leader in extraordinary times can be a lonely journey. It is a rare person who doesn't feel some degree of discomfort and anxiety in the face of uncertainty, ambiguity, and transition. As leaders, many of us have been taught to suck it up when guiding others through change. It is hard to argue with the power of positive thinking or the value of being strong and self-reliant. At the same time, however, you can supplement these personal strengths by drawing on the reservoir of support that resides in the experience and talents of others. Learning to trust those around us to provide meaningful input and just-in-time feedback is critical to the revitalization and recovery process. Learn to recognize when your own natural tendencies toward perfectionism or simply doing it yourself might be getting in the way of arriving at the best outcome. You are generally held accountable for getting things done right, but you are rarely charged with achieving those results single-handedly. Trusting others to carry a share of the load is a core element of effective transitional leadership.

Open up. Seek out a few trusted colleagues with whom you feel safe opening up about your work and your leadership role. Build a network of peers with whom it is comfortable and safe to go offline and dialogue. Use these connections to raise unresolved issues or to vent some of your personal frustrations. There is power in learning to be situationally vulnerable about fears, concerns, and mistakes. People expect their leaders to be strong, but they are also on the alert to determine whether their leaders are trying to play the role of Superman and pretending to be invincible.

Don't narrow your view. Cultivate diversity. In times of stress and uncertainty it is natural to gravitate toward those who share your strengths and see the world through the same lenses that you do. However, this is a time when you need to provide others with the opportunity to add value in ways that fall outside your own experience and comfort zone. Trust the good intentions of others unless they give you cause to do otherwise.

Listen to others. Create a safe place for others to speak truth to power. Leading during difficult times demands an open flow of both positive and negative feedback. Regular open forums can provide you with one vehicle for receiving honest input. Cultivating the informal channels may be even more effective. Block out some time each day to simply pause and listen to those out on the front lines.

	Overdone	Underdone
Self-Reliance	• Operates alone • Holds issues inside • Carries a heavy load • Narrows the options • Has trouble sharing • Can be a perfectionist	• Leaves things to chance • Doesn't follow through • Is timid • Doesn't inspire others • Is easily overwhelmed • Doesn't add value to the leadership process
Trusting Others	• Abdicates responsibility and authority • Trusts wrong people • Is often seen as naive • Reveals too much • Leaves groups leaderless • Is at risk with peers	• Second-guesses others • Hoards needed information • Stays detached or isolated • Stifles growth in others • Is a poor team builder • Has "silo" relationships

7

CAPITALIZING ON STRENGTHS VERSUS GOING AGAINST THE GRAIN

In times of crisis, people have a tendency to lock onto the strengths that have forged their success in the past. Capitalizing on strengths entails knowing one's strengths and attributes, and confidently relying on them to tackle new challenges. Someone who knows how to capitalize on strengths trusts the abilities that have generated success, rewards, recognition, compliments, and promotions in the past and uses them in new situations.

For experienced managers, it's easy to capitalize on strengths. They have a history of being rewarded for what they already know how to do and doing it in a way they already know how to do it. It is comfortable. But relying too much on strengths can cement leaders into behavior patterns that may no longer work. Failing to recognize conditions that demand different capacities and new learning can be disastrous. Sometimes it's necessary to leave one's comfort zone, challenge preferred patterns, and learn and try new things—in other words, to go against the grain.

As leaders gain experience and become more competent at a task or in their leadership roles, they also become more confident. But there may come a time when the strength is no longer sufficient or effective. To improve, they must change how they go about their work. Sometimes an external force changes the circumstances, and there is no choice but to do things differently. This going against the grain may pull you into awkwardness and doubt. It feels different. It is no longer typical. It is uncomfortable. At first, you are likely to be less effective applying the new way than you were with the old way. It's hard to set your strengths aside long enough to go against the grain—particularly when under pressure to make a change, to move the organization, to look good. You're under the spotlight, and you're being asked to take the organization to another place. It's much easier to fall back on what you—and those around you—already know. Yet to take the organization to another place often requires doing what you have not done before.

For all these reasons, we talk about this as the huge conspiracy in life to keep you doing what you already know how to do and the way you originally learned to do it. The first conspirator is you; the second conspirator is everyone else.

Leaders who overdo capitalizing on strengths while underdoing going against the grain create organizations that are averse to risk and not very resilient in difficult times. Often, they sacrifice the long term for the short term and ignore or resist new opportunities while maintaining the status quo.

When the reverse is true—underdoing capitalizing on strengths while overdoing going against the grain—there is not enough stability in the environment. These leaders are often described as loose cannons. They seem to like change for change's sake and tend to be indiscriminate in their change efforts: they discard the good along with the bad. In this environment, people feel fearful and at risk because their strengths and history are not valued.

By finding the appropriate balance between capitalizing on strengths and going against the grain, you foster the ability to learn. Openness to new ideas is balanced with a respect for experience and expertise. Leaders who achieve this balance pay attention to three critical things:

1. They accurately assess their strengths, weaknesses, preferences, and default behaviors. Authentic leadership is based on a clear sense of self. Self-awareness allows leaders to distinguish between habitual patterns and true strengths,

work to mitigate weaknesses, gain new skills, and practice different behaviors.

2. They seek out diversity. With an accurate sense of themselves, leaders can intentionally leverage the diverse talents, experiences, opinions, and perspectives of others. This helps prevent tunnel vision and groupthink.

3. They value learning. To do something new or to take on another perspective requires a willingness to learn. Authentic leaders value learning for themselves, their coworkers, and their organization. Without possessing and promoting a learning orientation, leaders are not likely to see the full potential of any change initiative.

Lillian, a senior manager in a company we've worked with, was widely viewed as loyal, effective, and efficient—but not at all creative or innovative. She oversaw an organization whose market share was 70 percent, and from her perspective, the way to maintain market leadership was to keep doing what had always been done. Several years ago, her boss said, "We're going to die if we don't rethink this market. We need to go to our customers and develop our product around their needs." For Lillian, this was a total reversal of the way they had successfully done business before. In addition, it would be her job to implement the turnaround. She had to motivate other people to change. To do so, she not only had to buy into the change but also had to let go of some of her strengths and some of the organization's strengths. Lillian was successful, in part, because she had a boss who pushed her, coached her, and held her accountable.

For Lillian, as with many leaders, the process of learning and growing as a leader was not a crisis or even marked by a single turning point. Rather, she understood that she needed to lead change and that doing so would require her to change too. By adjusting her mind-set and trying new behaviors over time, Lillian learned new ways to operate and has become a more balanced, flexible leader.

The next challenge for Lillian will be to lead this level of change on her own—to see how solidly the lessons learned over the last few years have taken hold. Her boss believes she's ready, saying that she has learned what she needed to learn to move to the next level—and take his place.

IN BALANCE

Capitalizing on Strengths ——— **TRUST** ——— Going against the Grain

Leaders who capitalize on their strengths

- ❏ focus on what they are good at and have experience with
- ❏ let others do what they are good at
- ❏ get people involved and engaged
- ❏ learn from people around them
- ❏ capture good ideas and stay open to them
- ❏ surround themselves with diversity and a wide range of character and experience
- ❏ acknowledge what they don't know
- ❏ focus attention on repeating successes
- ❏ exploit talent effectively in a diverse environment

Leaders who go against the grain

❏ are prepared to challenge assumptions for the sake of learning

❏ are not afraid of taking risks or making mistakes

❏ ask different and difficult questions that challenge the status quo

❏ challenge at the appropriate time and with the right amount of pressure

❏ engage others who will assist in going against the grain

❏ understand and define obstacles

❏ have a plan and objectives for moving forward

❏ understand the corporate culture and how it may hinder change

❏ operate with honesty and integrity

❏ are creative and entrepreneurial

Making It True

How can you strike a balance between capitalizing on your strengths and going against the grain? Here are some suggestions:

Pay attention to your patterns. Take time to systematically reflect on your lifelong learning history. Your goal is to gain a better sense of who you are and how you came to be that way. What are your key strengths? How applicable are they to your emerging environment? Which are most likely to become obsolete? What new strengths will you need in the changing marketplace? Pay attention as well to established flaws or weaknesses. You most likely have developed ways to compensate for these weaknesses in the present, but shifts in the demands of your environment could suddenly expose your vulnerability.

Leverage strengths intentionally. Understand your strengths and practice using them mindfully. When you default to your strengths, you lose opportunities for creativity and growth. Instead, ask yourself whether an approach or response is really the best way— or simply a habit.

Avoid complacency. Be purposeful in providing stretch assignments to team members. With too little stretch, people won't be pushed to go against the grain; with too much, they will seek comfort and confidence by reverting to prior strengths. Pair a new learner with a mentor or coach. Establish realistic deadlines for demonstrating that a new skill or behavior pattern has been implemented.

Value learning. Honor established practices but seek out incremental improvement to the process. Never allow yourself or those around you to become complacent enough to believe that they have fully arrived. Reward managers for developing others and supporting continuous learning. At some point, people will realize that the ability to learn is a core competency and that new strengths will always be required in a changing world.

Learn from failure. Create an environment where people sense that it is safe to debrief their failures as well as their successes. Focus more on how things are done rather than simply what was done. Comprehending the learning strategy and thought process behind our actions can be far more educational than dwelling on the outcomes.

Don't limit yourself or others. Seek out diversity, but be careful not to stereotype or pigeonhole people based on ethnicity, gender, field of study, and so on. Encourage group members to challenge and defend opposing points of view and take stands on major decisions. Rotate these roles so that no one individual is stigmatized with labels such as devil's advocate, naysayer, or Pollyanna.

Encourage new thinking. Honor and reward those who are willing to put time and energy into exploring novel problem solutions—even when their attempts might be viewed as incremental, expansive, tried before, rule challenging, or just plain stupid. Question people respectfully with the goal of mining any and all aspects of their ideas. Are there pieces, concepts, or perspectives that may shed new light on the current subject or other issues?

	Overdone	Underdone
Capitalizing on Strengths	• Is stagnant • Is stuck in prior learning • Misses uniqueness • Pigeonholes others • Jumps to the familiar • Resists needed change • Oversells past achievements	• Seeks too much stretch • Jumps to new challenges • Ignores stable tasks • Underutilizes strengths • Misses core objectives • Has no basis of ongoing success
Going against the Grain	• Plays the devil's advocate • Constantly explores but fails to take action • Makes change for change's sake • Doesn't persevere • Leads others in over their heads • Is too critical of the past	• Is stuck in old habits and patterns • May derail self or others • Doesn't model learning • Can be a yes-person • Doesn't add learning value to team

8
PLOTTING YOUR TENDENCIES

Throughout this book we suggest behaviors and ensuing perceptions on each of the dimensions of the transition leadership wheel. Each chapter gives you a chance to reflect on your own tendencies. Now we invite you to go back through the book, actually checking or highlighting your tendencies. Pull your intuitive reflections together, and examine how your tendencies on the different dimensions may interact. As with each chapter reflection, this is a very subjective exercise. It is difficult to quantify how much overdoing or underdoing is enough to have a negative impact on a leader's effectiveness. For example, how often do you need to express a sense of urgency (a necessary skill set) before your behavior crosses an invisible threshold and becomes a problem? How much overdoing of one dimension does it take to affect the corresponding dimension on the other side of the wheel? At this point you must rely on your subjective assessment of the impact of your behavior on others. Although this is not a quantitative measure, we are confident that most people intuitively know when the threshold has been crossed. Of course, it is much easier to see it in others than in ourselves. But honest self-reflection is the starting place for any significant development activity. The next (and bolder) step is to seek external feedback along these dimensions and compare it to your own assessment.

What follows is a simple worksheet for using the transition leadership wheel to examine your style. We encourage you to go back into the appropriate chapters and bring your self-reflections forward into this framework. For maximum learning it is best to examine each dimension independently. We will prompt you to do this from two perspectives: your own and others'. We want you to wonder how others might see you on the dimensions. Call upon any feedback you have received on related behavior. Are there any adjectives that people would attach to you that may inform you? What do they say about you when you are not around? It is not unusual that people may perceive you differently than you intend. We all think about the "correct" things, but busy schedules don't always allow us to get around to actually doing them. Because we've had the internal experience (thinking, imagining), we sometimes lose track of whether we have actually put our good ideas into action.

While each of the dimensions represents a critical leadership skill set, you should not expect to be operating on target on all of them. Your personality, preferences, and past experience all influence and shape your tendencies. For example, almost all of us are guilty of overdoing competencies that we are particularly good at or that have served us well in the past. These exceptions don't normally change the general perception in the eyes of others. There are other dimensions on which our behavior is more regular, more of a pattern that people associate with us. For this exercise we want you to respond to some prompts in terms of what you believe your dominant tendency is.

Assessing and Plotting Leadership Style

Please read the competency statements below and use the following response choices to capture your assessment of each statement. Then use the space provided to note the behaviors that cause you to rate yourself the way that you do.

O++ Overdo consistently and in multiple ways

O+ Overdo to a moderate degree with some residual negative impact

O Overdo occasionally to a slight degree, but not currently a problem

AR About right, neither underdo nor overdo

U Underdo occasionally to a slight degree, but not currently a problem

U- Underdo to a moderate degree with some residual negative impact

U-- Underdo consistently and in multiple ways

Catalyzing Change

Consistently promotes the cause. Encourages others to get on board and reinforces those who already are. Drives to get self and others engaged in any new initiative.

My self-rating

_____

Intentions and behaviors that underlie my self-rating:

_____

_____

_____

Perceptions of others; intentions and behaviors they attribute to me:

_____

_____

_____

Possible adjustments in my behavior to increase my effectiveness:

_____

_____

_____

Coping with Transition

*Is in touch with own reactions to change
and transition, and is comfortable sharing
those emotions. Walks the talk and leads by
example. Models coping behavior.*

My self-rating

_____

Intentions and behaviors that underlie my self-rating:

_____

_____

_____

Perceptions of others; intentions and behaviors they attribute
to me:

_____

_____

_____

Possible adjustments in my behavior to increase my
effectiveness:

_____

_____

_____

Sense of Urgency

Is an action person. Always looks to start the action and keep things rolling. Moves on issues quickly and pushes others to work at a rapid pace. Wants to get things done.

My self-rating

_____

Intentions and behaviors that underlie my self-rating:

_____

_____

_____

Perceptions of others; intentions and behaviors they attribute to me:

_____

_____

_____

Possible adjustments in my behavior to increase my effectiveness:

_____

_____

_____

Realistic Patience

Appreciates that people learn and cope with change differently and does not judge them based on his or her own style, preferences, or capabilities. Allows others the time and space to keep up.

My self-rating

_____

Intentions and behaviors that underlie my self-rating:

_____

_____

_____

Perceptions of others; intentions and behaviors they attribute to me:

_____

_____

_____

Possible adjustments in my behavior to increase my effectiveness:

_____

_____

_____

Being Tough

Makes the tough calls and difficult decisions about issues and people with little hesitation or second-guessing. Is not afraid to take a stand in the face of public opinion or strong resistance.

My self-rating

_____

Intentions and behaviors that underlie my self-rating:

_____

_____

_____

Perceptions of others; intentions and behaviors they attribute to me:

_____

_____

_____

Possible adjustments in my behavior to increase my effectiveness:

_____

_____

_____

Being Empathetic

Puts self in other people's shoes. Takes others' perspectives into account when taking action or implementing decisions. Gives others the benefit of the doubt.

My self-rating

_____

Intentions and behaviors that underlie my self-rating:

_____

_____

_____

Perceptions of others; intentions and behaviors they attribute to me:

_____

_____

_____

Possible adjustments in my behavior to increase my effectiveness:

_____

_____

_____

Optimism

Sees the upside and positive potential of any situation. Communicates and conveys that optimism to others.

My self-rating

_____

Intentions and behaviors that underlie my self-rating:

_____

_____

_____

Perceptions of others; intentions and behaviors they attribute to me:

_____

_____

_____

Possible adjustments in my behavior to increase my effectiveness:

_____

_____

_____

Realism and Openness

Is realistic and grounded in assessing prospects for the future. Is candid and open in communicating what is known and not known. Speaks the truth and doesn't sugar-coat the facts. Admits personal mistakes and foibles.

My self-rating

_____

Intentions and behaviors that underlie my self-rating:

_____

_____

_____

Perceptions of others; intentions and behaviors they attribute to me:

_____

_____

_____

Possible adjustments in my behavior to increase my effectiveness:

_____

_____

_____

Self-Reliance

Has a great deal of confidence in own skills and abilities, and is willing to step up and tackle new challenges. Is willing to take a lead role and do it himself or herself when necessary.

My self-rating

_____

Intentions and behaviors that underlie my self-rating:

_____

_____

_____

Perceptions of others; intentions and behaviors they attribute to me:

_____

_____

_____

Possible adjustments in my behavior to increase my effectiveness:

_____

_____

_____

Trusting Others

Is comfortable letting others do their part of a task or project. Is open to input and support from colleagues and friends. Shows respect for others and is willing to be vulnerable with them.

My self-rating

_____

Intentions and behaviors that underlie my self-rating:

_____

_____

_____

Perceptions of others; intentions and behaviors they attribute to me:

_____

_____

_____

Possible adjustments in my behavior to increase my effectiveness:

_____

_____

_____

Capitalizing on Strengths

Knows own strengths and attributes, and confidently relies on them to tackle new challenges. Trusts the abilities that have generated success, rewards, recognition, compliments, and promotions in the past.

My self-rating

_____

Intentions and behaviors that underlie my self-rating:

_____

_____

_____

Perceptions of others; intentions and behaviors they attribute to me:

_____

_____

_____

Possible adjustments in my behavior to increase my effectiveness:

_____

_____

_____

Going against the Grain
Is willing to try new things even when the new is difficult or painful. Can tolerate discomfort while learning.

My self-rating

_____

Intentions and behaviors that underlie my self-rating:

_____

_____

_____

Perceptions of others; intentions and behaviors they attribute to me:

_____

_____

_____

Possible adjustments in my behavior to increase my effectiveness:

_____

_____

_____

Now plot your self-ratings on the wheel on the next page (you may also download a copy of the wheel at www.ccl.org/wheel). For each of the twelve competencies, mark a dot along the spoke that best indicates your typical leadership behavior. The black line represents behavior that is about right. Moving out into the gray area is overdoing a competency, and moving into the white area is underdoing a competency. This will give you an intuitive—and fairly accurate—representation of whether your leadership is in true. Do you see the tensions between opposing spokes? Are some of your mental models about leadership conducive to leading in the constant change of contemporary organizational life?

Another interesting exercise is to plot your self-ratings in one color and the perceptions you think others have of you in another color. The differences between the two perspectives can be informing. Of course, the real test would be to take these reflections and share them with a trusted colleague.

You can also use the wheel to plot the leadership behaviors valued by your organization. If a leader performed only the behaviors rewarded by the organization, what would that profile look like? Comparing that profile to your self-ratings may help you recognize where your personal values and beliefs correspond or collide with those of your organization.

TRANSITION LEADERSHIP WHEEL

9

COMPLEXITIES THAT CHALLENGE BALANCE

In the preceding section and indeed throughout this book, we encourage you to be mindful of maintaining a dynamic tension between the opposing competencies of the model. It is certainly true that over time and across multiple situations we believe you will find greatest success by managing your behavior such that you operate near the midrange on each competency (neither overdoing nor underdoing consistently). Striking a balance will enhance your ability to cultivate trust and increase the likelihood that you will lead in an authentic fashion—particularly during times of change and transition. That being said, there are also times that call for the ability to manage "out of balance" in order to meet the demands of situational challenges—situational leadership, if you will. While a detailed examination of the more subtle application of the model is beyond the scope of this book, a couple of examples may serve to stimulate your thinking.

Situational Demands for Leadership

There are actually good reasons for managing with the competencies out of balance…at least for limited periods of time. Take, for example, the manager who inherited a division that had suffered from inattentive and lax leadership and had missed its targets for five quarters…more than a year underdelivering and exceeding budget. A change in management was made to correct the situation. The new manager came in and found poor levels of motivation and performance at lower levels in the division. There was a general lackadaisical attitude. People seemed totally unconcerned about their failure to meet objectives. Excuses for the poor performance were rampant, but data suggested low effort, poor attention to detail, and a general lack of urgency. The previous manager had exercised patience during the last reorganization, trying to allow people time to understand and accept the new strategy, but he had failed to balance that patience with the drive and motivation to follow through on the needed changes. Resistance and complacency had taken hold, and the change effort was being derailed.

The new manager had to ratchet up the sense of urgency in order to break the malaise and stimulate attention to productivity and better cost management. Although she understood that the change in leadership added yet another transition to be coped with, she also understood that her major challenge was to interrupt the negative and unhealthy behavior pattern that was presently blocking performance. She brought her team together and issued very challenging cost management and productivity targets. She explained the dilemma that the division was in and how it was affecting other parts of the company. She was careful to let her team members know that it should not have to be this way indefinitely, but that she would be monitoring more closely than usual until the division's contribution had been reestablished. She instituted more team meetings and shortened report times. She opened the door to input from the team, but didn't hesitate to rely on her own judgment and experience when swift action or decisions were required.

If you were to assess this leader's performance on the wheel during this turnaround period, you would likely rate her as overdoing sense of urgency, self-reliance, being tough, and catalyzing change, while limiting her expression of realistic patience and trusting others. These tactics were undertaken deliberately and consciously and were justified in the short term to reignite the change process. Typically, new managers will be granted a grace period while their approaches and styles are evaluated. We propose, however, that if this style of operating is tied more to personal preference than to situational demands or if it is maintained after the triggering situation has improved, the likely result will be a breakdown in morale and trust and a culture that operates on the basis of compliance rather than commitment. In the situation above, people might continue to meet the minimum requirements of her demands, but she would lose respect and trust to a degree that would likely undermine sustainable commitment and long-term success. Of course, this situation might have been avoided entirely had the leader's predecessor been more balanced in applying the wheel's competencies when the change was rolled out in the first place.

This is but one example of how some of the competencies may need increased or decreased emphasis in certain situations. A deeper examination of the subtle impact of cultural and situational forces is beyond the scope of this book. It has been our experience that managers have a tendency to overdo the more traditional competencies associated with leadership, such as being tough and self-reliance, over the aspects of emotional intelligence affiliated with being empathetic and trusting others. These patterns often appear to be linked to stereotypical mental models of how leaders are supposed to behave. The effect can be heightened when these same behavior patterns are subsequently reinforced by the reward systems in unenlightened organizational cultures. Neither is an excuse if the establishment of authentic leadership is the goal.

The ever-changing landscape of business makes it impossible for anyone to "settle in" on a balanced profile. The model is meant to be dynamic. It requires managers to periodically assess themselves on the competencies. The circumstances at the time will determine which of the competencies may need more or less emphasis. If managers find that they are habitually overdoing or underdoing the same competencies, it may be helpful for them to search for unintended consequences that may have escaped their attention. It is these unintended consequences that separate the mediocre from the excellent.

Prevailing Leadership Culture

Throughout this book we have characterized the expression of the various dimensions of the transition leadership wheel as though they were the unique province of an individual's preferred leadership style or typical pattern of behavior. Indeed, we know from our work with thousands of executives that the tendency to overdo or underdo a given competency (or cluster of related competencies) is often linked to the presence of underlying personality characteristics, interpersonal needs and values, or prior learning experiences. On the other hand, understanding and predicting leadership behavior is a bit more complex than that. Simply stated, a given leader's behavior never exists in a vacuum. Every organization has a culture that helps to shape and define the context in which an individual's behavior is perceived and judged. The emphasis a leader gives the different competencies of the wheel is influenced by the organization's culture, and the formal and informal reward systems that reinforce that culture. Often the most powerful factors are subtle and difficult to observe unless one is part of the system. The powerful rules that drive and hone leader behavior are often the unwritten and unspoken threads that are woven into the fabric of day-to-day life. People come to know these subtleties by how they are rewarded or punished. The rewards and punishments are themselves often subtle. They shape behavior and are most powerful (and sometimes insidious) when they are outside our awareness.

For example, some organizational cultures operate in a heavy-handed and competitive manner with little room for mistakes and no patience with the expression of discontent. Such an organization might be perceived as a dog-eat-dog, survival-of-the-fittest kind of place. This information, of course, would never show up in the mission statement, employee handbook, or formal orientation session. People figure it out from the way some people with certain styles or patterns of strengths are recognized and favored while others are passed over and discounted. These norms are revealed in how the leaders act day to day. Their behavior serves as a model for how others are supposed to act in their own practice of leadership.

We were once brought in to coach a very promising assistant vice president by the human resources department. He had been accused of abusive behavior in general and of creating a toxic environment in his department. After meeting with him, conducting some psychological assessments, and interviewing people close to him, we found a person whose intentions and style seemed to be at odds with the negative behavior attributed to him. In our coaching sessions we discovered that he was acting not in congruence with his own beliefs and style, but was instead repeating patterns of behavior that he had witnessed in other leaders in the company. While he was never directly encouraged to treat people in such a negative way, he had learned to operate in that fashion by observing others being rewarded for that style. We offer this example as neither an excuse for ineffective leadership behavior nor an example of executive naïveté. Rather, our purpose is to demonstrate the subtle and insidious ways that organizational culture can influence leadership behavior and style.

It is important to remember that cultural norms can transmit effective, healthy patterns of behavior as well. When conducting organizational assessment interviews within organizations, we often find leaders who are modeling behavior that is both engaging and motivating. When asked why they do what they do, they might say,

"I really hadn't thought about it. It's just the way we do things here." Admittedly, we are more likely to be invited into situations where leaders need to shift their behavior in a positive direction. But we would be remiss if we failed to acknowledge that organizational culture can operate in ways that nurture and support the practice of effective leadership rather than undermine it.

What are the subtle ways that your organizational culture operates to influence leader behavior? A useful exercise is to map those subtleties on the transition leadership wheel. Can you actually name some of the influences? Can you see how your culture may influence your leadership style? Can you catch yourself passing some of those influences along to those who look to you for leadership?

It is less than authentic leadership to blame your culture for your behavior. Yes, it is a challenge to behave in ways that are in conflict with the prevailing cultural norms. It may appear easier and safer to simply conform to the practices observed in others, but accepting the leadership challenge includes being willing to challenge practices that aren't in the best interest of the organization or its constituents. It takes more courage to follow one's own beliefs and values than to fall into the pace and style of an organization's culture. And in the end, most leaders will find that their careers are judged and rewarded based on their competence, their performance, and their personal integrity. Leading with authenticity—balancing the dynamic tensions between the human and structural aspects of leadership—can be the most effective. If your culture rewards and punishes leadership behavior in a manner that fosters chronic imbalance and you succumb to that style, you may thrive in the short term while undermining your ultimate potential as a leader in the long term. Leading with authenticity will often test your level of personal conviction, but you will never have the ease of applying your own style within a vacuum. Cultural context will always be present.

APPENDIX: AND THE WORK CONTINUES...

Our growing understanding of how authenticity enriches leadership was born from practice. We have had countless conversations, from formal interviews to casual chats, with leaders living through significant organizational turmoil. We have worked with more than two thousand leaders in a feedback-intensive, weeklong training program titled Leading People through Transition. We have provided coaching to many individual managers trying to cope. We listened. They taught us. Through the lens of various models of leadership, organizational development, and adult learning, the current model has emerged.

There has been much anecdotal evidence to support the contention that the issues outlined in this book make a difference. However, consistent with CCL's commitment to the study of leadership, we are engaged in continued research in this arena. There is an organizational impact study under way with one of the organizations that trained more than six hundred leaders with our program. Development of a 360-degree feedback tool is also under way. Items have been written and vetted with three hundred managers from around the globe. Research test sites are being set up with a variety of companies who are interested in joining us on our journey. We are collaborating with organizations, practitioners, and research colleagues who are also interested and doing similar work. If you are interested in having your organization participate in this research, please check the CCL Web site (www.ccl.org) for current information.

SUGGESTED READINGS

Baldwin, D., & Grayson, C. (2004). *Influence: Gaining commitment, getting results.* Greensboro, NC: Center for Creative Leadership.

Bridges, W. (2001). *The way of transition: Embracing life's most difficult moments.* Cambridge, MA: Perseus Publishing.

Bridges, W. (2004). *Transitions: Making sense of life's changes* (2nd ed.). Cambridge, MA: Da Capo Press.

Buckingham, M. (2005). *The one thing you need to know . . . about great managing, great leading, and sustained individual success.* New York: Free Press.

Bunker, K. A. (1997). The power of vulnerability in contemporary leadership. *Consulting Psychology Journal: Practice and Research, 49*(2), 122–136.

Bunker, K. A., & Wakefield, M. (2004). In search of authenticity: Now more than ever, soft skills are needed. *Leadership in Action, 24*(1), 16–20.

Collins, J. C. (2001). *Good to great: Why some companies make the leap . . . and others don't.* New York: HarperBusiness.

Covey, S. R. (2004). *The 8th habit: From effectiveness to greatness.* New York: Free Press.

Dalton, M. A. (1998). *Becoming a more versatile learner.* Greensboro, NC: Center for Creative Leadership.

George, B. (2003). *Authentic leadership: Rediscovering the secrets to creating lasting value.* San Francisco: Jossey-Bass.

Gurvis, J., & Patterson, G. (2004). *Finding your balance.* Greensboro, NC: Center for Creative Leadership.

Johnson, B. (1992). *Polarity management: Identifying and managing unsolvable problems.* Amherst, MA: HRD Press.

Kaplan, R. E. (1999). *Internalizing strengths: An overlooked way of overcoming weaknesses in managers.* Greensboro, NC: Center for Creative Leadership.

Kirkland, K., & Manoogian, S. (1998). *Ongoing feedback: How to get it, how to use it.* Greensboro, NC: Center for Creative Leadership.

Klann, G. (2003). *Crisis leadership: Using military lessons, organizational experiences, and the power of influence to lessen the impact of chaos on the people you lead.* Greensboro, NC: Center for Creative Leadership.

Kouzes, J. M., & Posner, B. Z. (1993). *Credibility: How leaders gain and lose it, why people demand it.* San Francisco: Jossey-Bass.

Kouzes, J. M., & Posner, B. Z. (2002). *The leadership challenge* (3rd ed.). San Francisco: Jossey-Bass.

Kubler-Ross, E. (1997). *On death and dying.* New York: Scribner Classics.

McCall, M. W. (1998). *High flyers: Developing the next generation of leaders.* Boston: Harvard Business School Press.

Noer, D. M. (1993). *Healing the wounds: Overcoming the trauma of layoffs and revitalizing downsized organizations.* San Francisco: Jossey-Bass.

Pulley, M. L. (1997). *Losing your job—reclaiming your soul: Stories of resilience, renewal, and hope.* San Francisco: Jossey-Bass.

Pulley, M. L., & Wakefield, M. (2001). *Building resiliency: How to thrive in times of change.* Greensboro, NC: Center for Creative Leadership.

Reina, D. S., & Reina, M. L. (1999). *Trust and betrayal in the workplace: Building effective relationships in your organization.* San Francisco: Berrett-Koehler Publishers.

Scott, C. D., & Jaffe, D. T. (with Raulston, N. C.). (1997). *Take this work and love it.* Menlo Park, CA: Crisp Publications.

Senge, P. M. (1990). *The fifth discipline: The art and practice of the learning organization.* New York: Doubleday.

Shaw, R. B. (1997). *Trust in the balance: Building successful organizations on results, integrity, and concern.* San Francisco: Jossey-Bass.

Terry, R. W. (1993). *Authentic leadership: Courage in action.* San Francisco: Jossey-Bass.

Weitzel, S. R. (2000). *Feedback that works: How to build and deliver your message.* Greensboro, NC: Center for Creative Leadership.

Other CCL Press Fieldbooks

Crisis Leadership
Using Military Lessons, Organizational Experiences, and the Power of Influence to Lessen the Impact of Chaos on the People You Lead

Nothing tests a leader like a crisis. There is an element of the leader's deepest character that is revealed during highly charged, dramatic events. A crisis can quickly expose a leader's hidden strengths and core weaknesses. It can show the world if the leader has what it takes to function effectively when the heat is on. Will the leader address the crisis head-on, take those actions needed to fix it, and, if appropriate, take responsibility for the crisis? Will the leader freeze, or worse, claim to be a victim and pass off the responsibility to others? What can and should a leader do to find out what went wrong and to ensure it doesn't happen again?

Three leadership elements have a tremendous impact on crisis leadership. These elements—communication, clarity of vision and values, and caring relationships—are important to leaders in normal operations, but their importance is magnified during a crisis. By paying attention to these themes, leaders can hope to increase their understanding of practices that handle the human dimension of a crisis. The result is a leader more prepared to contain the crisis, regain control of the situation, ensure the minimum amount of damage is done to the organization, and effectively prevent, defuse, and reduce the duration of these extremely difficult leadership situations.

The anxiety, insecurity, and confusion that a crisis generates are huge challenges for leaders. They must be prepared to provide leadership not only to those in their organization, but also to those in the greater orbit of their influence: clients and customers, the surrounding community, stockholders, suppliers, vendors, local government, concerned organizations, activist groups, and the media. And, of course, leaders must also lead themselves. They must deal with their own emotions and needs a crisis triggers. For some leaders, this may be the biggest challenge of all. (CCL Stock No. 185)

Evaluating the Impact of Leadership Development: A Professional Guide

Scratch the surface of any successful organization and you'll likely find systems designed to evaluate how well it runs. Commercial and not-for-profit organizations use evaluation processes to weigh options, balance trade-offs, and make better decisions. An evaluation system gives organizations a logical and practical framework for collecting and assimilating information.

Although many professionals do difficult and excellent work in and with organizations to build leadership capacity, tools for supporting the evaluation of leadership development are few and far between. CCL's experience evaluating leadership development initiatives has given us specific ideas for how that work should be conceived and conducted: that it should be participatory, be integrated with initiative design, and enhance organizational learning.

Ideally, the focus and design of an evaluation are tightly integrated with the design of the initiative itself. When collaborative processes are used to focus the evaluation and to apply the results and evaluation work is integrated into the design and implementation of an initiative, both the initiative and the evaluation are more effective, and organizational learning can result.

That learning gives organizations increased knowledge regarding barriers to and facilitators of organizational change. They learn which processes, structures, areas, or systems can support change, as well as what needs further attention. In addition, roles and responsibilities are further clarified during the evaluation planning process, which also includes strategies for sharing results and lessons across the organization.

Well-designed developmental initiatives link different kinds of learning opportunities and occur over a period of time. They also link individual development to organizational goals in a cycle of assessment, practice, and learning. The results of such initiatives are best measured with an evaluation process that is itself cyclical. Recognizing the cyclical nature of evaluations allows organizations to use them as planning and learning tools that augment the individual and group impact of leadership development. (CCL Stock No. 187)

Ordering Information

For more information, to order other CCL Press publications, or to find out about bulk-order discounts, please contact us by phone at 336-545-2810 or visit our online bookstore at **www.ccl.org/publications**. Prepayment is required for all orders under $100.

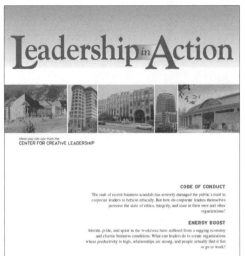

ideas you can use from the
CENTER FOR CREATIVE LEADERSHIP

CODE OF CONDUCT

The rash of recent business scandals has severely damaged the public's trust in corporate leaders to behave ethically. But how do corporate leaders themselves perceive the state of ethics, integrity, and trust in their own and other organizations?

ENERGY BOOST

Morale, pride, and spirit in the workforce have suffered from a sagging economy and chaotic business conditions. What can leaders do to create organizations where productivity is high, relationships are strong, and people actually find it fun to go to work?

POWER PLAY

By mobilizing the energy that exists in the collective knowledge and talents of the members of their teams, leaders can marshal the human, informational, and material resources needed to get things done.

VOLUME 24, NUMBER 4
SEPTEMBER/OCTOBER 2004

Leadership in Action

A publication of the
Center for Creative Leadership and Jossey-Bass

Leadership in Action is a bimonthly publication that aims to help practicing leaders and those who train and develop practicing leaders by providing them with insights gained in the course of CCL's educational and research activities. It also aims to provide a forum for the exchange of information and ideas between practitioners and CCL staff and associates.

To order, please contact Customer Service, Jossey-Bass, 989 Market Street, San Francisco, CA 94103-1741. Telephone: 888-378-2537; fax: 415-951-8553. See the Jossey-Bass Web site, at www.josseybass.com.